TOP
SECRET
FILES

The *American Revolution*

# TOP SECRET FILES

# The American Revolution

## STEPHANIE BEARCE

PRUFROCK PRESS INC.
WACO, TEXAS

Prufrock Press Inc.
P.O. Box 8813
Waco, TX 76714-8813
Phone: (800) 998-2208
Fax: (800) 240-0333
http://www.prufrock.com

# Table of Contents

## Secret Weapons

## Secret Forces

# Secrets

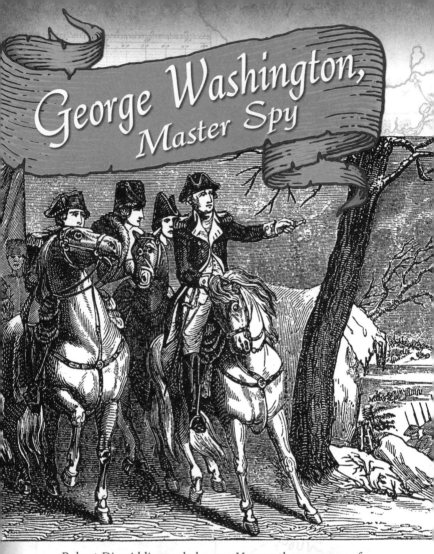

# George Washington, Master Spy

Robert Dinwiddie needed a spy. He was the governor of the British Colony of Virginia, and in 1753, it was his responsibility to protect the king's land from being taken over by the French. He had reports that the French were stirring up trouble out on the frontier. They were teaming up with Indians to raid and burn English settlers' cabins. They were stealing British guns and ammunition. Governor Dinwiddie was afraid the French were gearing up for war. He needed a spy to find out exactly what was going on.

One volunteer showed up to apply for the job. It was George Washington. At that time, he was not quite 21 years old and had already been given the rank of major in the Virginia militia. It was an amazingly high rank for someone so young, but Washington was an amazing man.

At 6 feet 3 inches tall, he towered over the other men of his day. The average height of a man in 1776 was 5 feet 8 inches, so Washington was 7 inches taller than most of his soldiers. Add that to the fact that he had bright red hair, and Washington stood out in a crowd. That's not what made him special or a good candidate for a spy, though.

It was Washington's experience and knowledge of the countryside that was so important. From the time he was 16, he had studied and worked as a land surveyor. He was an expert at making and reading maps. He spent weeks living in the wild while he surveyed the country, and he knew how to defend himself. In addition, he had a talent for understanding people and convincing them to do what he wanted. That was an excellent skill set for a spy.

At 6 feet 3 inches tall, he towered over the other men of his day. The average height of a man in 1776 was 5 feet 8 inches, so Washington was 7 inches taller than most of his soldiers.

Governor Dinwiddie immediately put Washington to work. Dinwiddie had an official letter for Washington to deliver to the French on the frontier, demanding that the French immediately vacate all lands.

Neither Washington nor the governor thought that the French would actually comply with the letter, but it would give Washington an official reason for being in the territory, and he could see if the French were planning to go to war with the British.

Washington had the information he needed. He immediately led his group back to Virginia and Governor Dinwiddie. The governor was thrilled with all of the information Washington brought back.

Before Washington set out for the frontier, he put together his own team of helpers, or operatives. He hired Christopher Gist as a guide. Gist knew the frontier well and could speak several native languages, so he would be Washington's interpreter for the Indians. Washington hired his longtime friend Jacob Van Braam (a sword master and mercenary who trained a teenage Washington) to be the French interpreter, and he hired four experienced traders who were friendly with the Indian populations.

The party set out for Ohio territory, not knowing for certain where they would find the French military or how many soldiers were there. They traveled through heavy rains, snow, and flooded rivers through the Allegheny Mountains to a settlement where Pittsburgh is now located. There they met a Seneca Indian chief who disliked the French and was quite willing to tell Washington and his party everything he knew about their troops and military.

After spending time in the village, some of the Seneca men led Washington to a house that had belonged to an English trader, but had been taken over by the French. Washington and his men rode up and started a friendly conversation with the French men, who were happy to meet the travelers. They eventually invited Washington's party to supper.

During the evening, the French soldiers brought out their wine and kept pouring more and more drinks until they were quite drunk. Washington just took tiny sips of his wine and refused any more so he stayed sober and alert.

Washington got the men talking about their plans. They told him that the French did indeed plan to take over the Ohio territory and had already built four forts that housed 150 soldiers each. Washington told them about the letter he carried

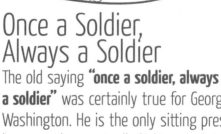

# Once a Soldier, Always a Soldier

The old saying **"once a soldier, always a soldier"** was certainly true for George Washington. He is the only sitting president known to have actually led troops into battle. During the **Whiskey Rebellion of 1794**, Washington personally traveled to Western Pennsylvania to take charge of the army and put down the protest.

telling them to vacate the land, and the soldiers just laughed. They said if the British wanted the land, they could try to come and take it.

The next morning, as Washington left, he noticed a large number of canoes. He quietly counted 50 birch bark and 170 pine canoes, with several more still to be carved out. Washington was sure that the French were planning to send their soldiers out to attack any British who were in the territory.

Washington had the information he needed. He immediately led his group back to Virginia and Governor Dinwiddie. The governor was thrilled with all of the information Washington brought back. He ordered Washington to write a full report to King George II. Washington used notes from his journal to write a 7,400-word report that was published in London. The report made Washington famous in England as well as in the colonies. It helped convince England to fight France for control of the territory and was the start of the French and Indian War.

The skills Washington learned during his time as a spy would come in handy when the colonies decided to strike out on their own and fight the war for independence from Britain. The next time, Washington would be managing the spies in a fight for the new country of America.

Map of Mount Vernon, residence of George Washington, made by himself, 1793

# The Boston Tea Party

The people of the American colonies
were fed up with King George III and
his ever-increasing tax demands.

The cold December wind whistled through the bare tree branches and a few stars poked through the dark sky. Whooping war chants filled the air while 200 men gathered by the Boston Harbor. It was the perfect night for a party, but not the kind you might think.

The people of the American colonies were fed up with King George III and his ever-increasing tax demands. They had endured the Stamp Act and the Townshend Acts, through which the English Parliament had imposed taxes on the American colonies, without allowing the colonies to elect representatives to Parliament. The colonists argued that these acts created "taxation without representation," which went against the laws of England.

But Parliament and King George told the colonists that they had every right to tax the Americans. After all, King George had his army stationed in America to protect them. His ships brought them goods, so of course, they should pay taxes on them. And to make that point perfectly clear, he decided to tax their favorite beverage—tea.

A huge protest was held, with 7,000 colonists in Boston yelling and arguing against the king's tea tax. They demanded that the ships carrying the tea return to England with none of the taxes paid. But Massachusetts Governor Thomas Hutchinson was loyal to King George and refused to let the ships leave their harbor. This made the colonists even angrier.

On the night of December 16, 1773, protestors known as the Sons of Liberty dressed themselves in Mohawk Indian costumes. They covered their faces with coal dust so they would not be recognized, and they attacked the three English ships

## Two Tea Parties?

Many people don't realize that there were actually two Boston Tea Parties, and there were also tea parties in other colonial cities. Three months after the original tea party, people were still angry, so they raided the British ship *Fortune* and dumped 30 more chests of tea into Boston Harbor. Patriots in New York, Annapolis, and Charleston, SC, also held tea parties of their own.

# Rotten Harbor

What happens to a harbor when you dump 92,000 pounds of tea in it? It stinks. For weeks after the Tea Party, the residents of Boston had to put up with the horrible smell of rotting tea leaves. And to keep looters from salvaging the tea that was floating in the harbor, members of the Sons of Liberty would go out in boats and hit the tea with oars to make it sink.

that carried the shipments of tea. They screamed war yells like the Native Americans and carried tomahawks and axes. The costumes were a symbol that the colonists identified themselves with the Native Americans and not with the English crown.

Two hundred men swarmed three ships: *Dartmouth*, *Eleanor*, and *Beaver*. They took the keys from the ships' captains, broke into the storage areas, and hacked open the chests of tea. Then they dumped the tea into Boston Harbor. There would be no taxes paid to King George and no money for the tea merchants. It was a huge act of defiance and set the colonists one step closer to revolution. It also ended the American love of tea. After the Boston Tea Party, it was considered unpatriotic to drink tea, so Americans switched to drinking coffee. They were still drinking coffee when the American Revolution started in 1776.

# Culper Spy Ring

Anna Strong lugged the heavy basket of wet clothes out to the backyard. She picked up a black petticoat and pinned it to the line. She then carefully selected four handkerchiefs and hung them up next to the petticoat. It was a simple act, but if she were caught she would be killed for treason.

Anna was a member of the Culper Spy Ring, and she used her laundry to send messages to Caleb Brewster on his boat. The black petticoat told Brewster there was a message to pick up and the number of handkerchiefs indicated in which of the six nearby coves he would find the message or package.

The Culper Ring reported directly to General George Washington and operated for 5 years without a single one of its spies being caught. It was perhaps the most important spy network in the American Revolution because it gave information to Washington about the British movements in New York City—an area that was under complete British control, except for the amazing Culper Spy Ring.

The Culper Spy Ring began when Benjamin Tallmadge was selected by George Washington to recruit spies in New York. At the time, Tallmadge was a 22-year-old major in the Continental Army and had grown up on Long Island, NY. As a patriot, he resented the British takeover of his hometown and was willing to do anything to get rid of the British rule.

Tallmadge was introduced to George Washington by General Charles Scott. At a secret meeting, the three men made plans for developing a spy ring in New York with Tallmadge as the head of the ring. It was George Washington who suggested the name Culper Spy Ring. Culper was a variation of Culpeper County, VA, where Washington had spent time working as a surveyor.

Washington's own experiences as a spy had shown him how important it was to protect the identities of the people doing the intelligence work. He told Tallmadge to use codes and code names to protect the patriot spies. Washington cared about the people working for him and did not want them to be imprisoned or executed.

Tallmadge's code name was John Bolton, and all of his correspondence with General Washington was under that name. Washington and Tallmadge devised a system of number codes, too. The number 711 was the code for General Washington, 745 was England, and 727 meant New York.

The first person Tallmadge recruited to be a spy was his childhood friend, Abraham Woodhull. Woodhull's spy name was Samuel Culper. Woodhull was a farmer on Long Island, and he would often visit his sister, who ran a boarding house in Manhattan. While there, he would spy on the British soldiers and talk with people in town to learn what was happening. When he returned to his farm, he would give his messages to Caleb Brewster, who was a whaleboat operator and another member of the Culper Spy Ring. Brewster sailed across Long Island Sound to deliver the messages to Tallmadge, who then delivered them to George Washington.

The British became suspicious because Woodhull seemed to be visiting his sister so much. Other reports noted that Woodhull would wander the city more than seemed reasonable, when he should have been with his sister. They sent the

# Not the Only Game in Town

The Culper Spy Ring was not the only spy game in the business. The first colonial spy ring was the **Mersereau ring**. It was started in 1776 by Staten Island shipyard owner Joshua Mersereau. Also, the **Clark Spy Ring** operated behind enemy lines in Philadelphia during 1777. It was because of the **success of these two rings** that Washington started the Culper Spy Ring.

Queen's Rangers to Woodhull's house to try to catch him with secret messages, but Woodhull was not home, so the Queen's Rangers attacked his father. Woodhull's father survived, but Washington and Tallmadge knew they needed to increase the number of spies to protect Woodhull and keep the information flowing.

During the next 5 years, Tallmadge recruited more friends and family to help with the spying. Austin Roe was a tavern keeper in Setauket who volunteered to serve as a messenger. During his trips to Manhattan to buy supplies, he carried messages and information. Robert Townsend was a shopkeeper in Manhattan, and he became known as Samuel Culper, Jr. His information helped stop a British plot to ruin the colonies' economy by printing counterfeit money. Abraham Woodhull's sister joined the spy ring, as did Robert Townsend's sister, Sally. George Smith, another whaleboat sailor, also helped Caleb Brewster.

The members of the spy ring wrote their messages either in code or with invisible ink. That way, if their messages fell into the hands of the British, they would not be understood. Often they wrote what seemed like a normal letter, but between the lines, the spies wrote with invisible ink, or they hid coded numbers and words in a shopping list or merchant ledger.

Nobody knows for sure how many people served as members of the Culper Spy Ring, and that is a testament to its success. The best spies are the ones who are never discovered. And that means the Culper Spy Ring included some of the very best. The public did not learn about the Culper Spy Ring until the 1930s. It took historians more than 150 years of studying letters and handwriting to learn that Robert Townsend was Culper, Jr. And the identity of agent 355 (only recognized as "lady" by the code used by Tallmadge) is still not known.

## SPY TRAINING

# Crack George's Code

George Washington created a very elaborate code system for use by the Culper spies. To understand any message, the reader had to have a codebook. See if you can interpret the message below using part of Washington's codebook.

**Message:**

220    657    711    500    625    635

**Codebook:**

| | | |
|---|---|---|
| 635 troops | 184 farm | 596 secret |
| 390 mischief | 605 summer | 546 riot |
| 174 express | 657 visit | 341 January |
| 721 John Bolton | 65 bounty | 711 Gen. Washington |
| 504 promote | 289 island | 722 Sam Culper |
| 220 go | 500 prepare | 219 gun |
| 110 company | 132 danger | 190 find |
| 634 to | 625 the | 628 these |

*(Answer: Go visit Gen. Washington, prepare the troops)*

George Washington also had a substitution code for the alphabet. You can use his code to write your own secret messages. You just need to make sure that you give your spy partner a copy of the code.

### George Washington's Alphabet Code

| | | |
|---|---|---|
| A = e | B = f | C = g |
| D = h | E = i | F = j |
| G = a | H = b | I = c |
| J = d | K = o | L = m |
| M= n | N = p | O = q |
| P = r | Q = k | R = l |
| S = u | T = v | U = w |
| V = x | W = y | X = z |
| Y = s | Z = t | |

You can look at Washington's complete code at http://www.mountvernon.org/george-washington/the-revolutionary-war/washington-spymaster/george-washington-spymaster/the-culper-code-book/

Use the space below to write your own secret message.

_____

_____

_____

_____

_____

_____

_____

_____

_____

_____

_____

_____

_____

_____

_____

_____

_____

_____

_____

_____

_____

## SPY TRAINING

# Tea Party Experiment

You may wonder why the Sons of Liberty had problems sinking the tea in the Boston Harbor. You can learn for yourself how difficult it is to sink tea with a simple experiment.

**Materials**

- ❑ 5 or 6 tea bags
- ❑ Glass of cold water
- ❑ Spoon

Carefully open the tea bags and dump the contents into the glass of water. Do the tea leaves sink or float?

Stir the water with the spoon. Try to get as much tea as possible to sink to the bottom of the glass. Then leave the glass alone for 5 minutes. When you return, check to see where the tea leaves are now. Imagine having an entire harbor full of thousands of pounds of tea leaves!

Spies

# Nathan Hale

Nathan Hale stood in a row with the other officers. They had all been summoned to Lieutenant Colonel Thomas Knowlton's office for a secret meeting. The colonel quietly explained that a volunteer was needed to gather information on the position and strength of the British troops in Manhattan, NY.

In September of 1776, New York City was a stronghold of the British. Thousands of soldiers lived and worked in the area, and it was an important port for obtaining supplies. If the British took over all of New York, it would be extremely difficult for the American colonies to win their independence. It was a critical mission. It was also a dangerous mission. Anyone caught spying on the British would be hanged.

The room filled with an uneasy silence. None of the young officers stepped forward. The colonel was not surprised. Most gentlemen of the 1700s considered spying to be dirty work and not an activity that gentlemen should be involved in. It was work for lower class, less educated men.

But the colonel was under direct orders from General George Washington to find a well-educated soldier who could bring them critical information. The colonel asked again for a volunteer. Nathan Hale stepped forward.

Hale was born in Coventry, CT, and was the sixth of 12 children born to his parents, Richard and Elizabeth Hale. At the age of 14, Nathan and his 16-year-old brother Enoch were sent to Yale College. Even though he was only 14, Nathan excelled in his studies and graduated with honors at the age of 18. He worked as a schoolteacher for 3 years until the Revolutionary War began in 1775, when he joined a Connecticut militia and eventually became a first lieutenant in the 7th Connecticut Regiment.

As he stood before Colonel Knowlton, Hale knew he had never served in a real battle. He had never even been to New York and he had certainly never done any spying, but young Nathan Hale believed in the freedom of America. He had received a letter from a Yale classmate that convinced him that he should do whatever it took to defend America.

> He had never even been to New York and he had certainly never done any spying, but young Nathan Hale believed in the freedom of America.

Hale respected his friend Benjamin Tallmadge's words, "Our holy Religion, the honor of our God, a glorious country, and a happy constitution is what we have to defend."

Colonel Knowlton was worried about Hale's lack of experience, but Hale was the only officer brave enough to volunteer. He was given maps of New York City and told to avoid talking to strangers. Hale was to use his experience as a schoolteacher as his cover identity. He was to pretend to be an out-of-work teacher looking for a job. There was only one problem. It was September, and school had already started. Still, Colonel Knowlton felt like it would be easier if Hale tried to keep as close to the truth as possible.

On September 12, Hale was secretly ferried across the water from Stamford, CT, to Long Island. There he was supposed to start talking to people in the area about teaching jobs and secretly take note of the numbers of British troops and their arms. But by the time Hale arrived, it was already too late. Just 3 days after Hale landed, the British captured Manhattan. Nathan Hale was trapped behind enemy lines.

Immediately his mission changed. Now instead of gathering information on how America could defend its last stronghold in New York, Hale had to try to get information on how they could win back the city.

Both Colonel Knowlton and General Washington were worried about their young spy. He had no experience. What if someone from his college days recognized him and told his real name and that he was an officer in the American Army? Anyone who could recognize Hale was a threat to his safety.

Hale remained in New York City, spying and taking notes for 8 days, but on September 20, Hale was captured by British soldiers who discovered his notes and drawings. He was declared a spy and was immediately sentenced to death by hanging.

Hale knew he was going to die. He had known it was real possibility when he took the job as a spy. After all, at the time, spies were hanged as illegal combatants. As he waited overnight in the British jail, he requested two things: a Bible and a visit from a pastor. Both were denied.

# Where Was Nathan Hale Hanged?

Nathan Hale is most commonly thought to have lost his life at the Park of Artillery, **located at modern-day 66th Street and Third Avenue in Manhattan**. However, at least six other sites in Manhattan have laid claim to being his last location, including City Hall Park and the Yale Club near Grand Central Station. Still other reports lay claim to **three different locations being the place where he was captured and four different spots being the place he was held until his execution.** With many accounts of history including contrasting details and the fact that Hale's remains have never been recovered, it's hard to know for sure where he may have met his fate.

Early on the morning of September 21, Nathan Hale was led to the gallows. As was the custom of the time, he was asked if he had any last words. According to eyewitness accounts, Hale stood bravely before the crowd of English soldiers and said these now famous words: "I only regret that I have but one life to lose for my country."

The news of Hale's death deeply affected Knowlton and Washington. They had been afraid that young Hale was too inexperienced, and now they knew he had paid for his bravery with his life.

# Hero to Zero
## Benedict Arnold

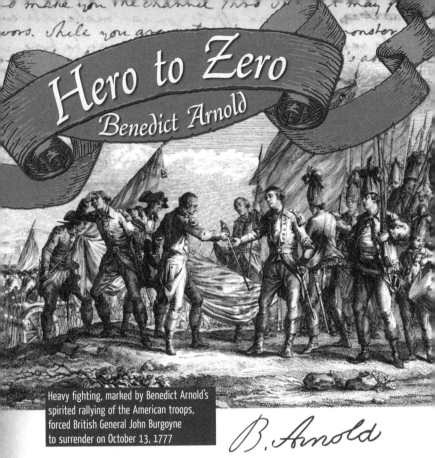

Heavy fighting, marked by Benedict Arnold's spirited rallying of the American troops, forced British General John Burgoyne to surrender on October 13, 1777

*B. Arnold*

Smoke from cannons and guns filled the air in Saratoga, NY, as British Redcoats attacked the American rebels. The fighting was hard and furious. The Americans were determined to route the British from the area and get closer to taking back New York, but the British were strong and experienced soldiers. The Americans had old weapons and limited ammunition.

Then, in the middle of the smoke and gunfire, an American officer bravely rode his horse to the front lines. His saber flashing and slashing, he yelled for the soldiers to fight for their country and their freedom. Up and down the line he charged, encouraging the troops while dodging gunshots and swords. The men saw his bravery and followed as he attacked from one angle and then another. He raced his horse from one side of the battlefield to the other, only stopping when a bullet shattered his leg. His men were so inspired that they drove the superior British forces out of Saratoga and helped secure that part of New York for the Americans.

It was an important victory not only because the Americans gained ground, but also because their victory convinced the French that the Americans could win the war with their help—leading them to send their troops to help the Americans fight the revolution. And that brave officer? He became famous as the hero of Saratoga. His name was Benedict Arnold.

Three years later, in 1870, General Benedict Arnold had become disgruntled with the Continental Congress. Arnold felt that nobody truly gave him credit for all of his hard work and sacrifice. The bullet that shattered his leg had left him crippled so that he walked with a limp. It also ended his combat career. He believed the Continental Congress had promoted other officers who didn't deserve it as much as he did and that other officers were taking credit for his accomplishments. Arnold was angry and wanted to get revenge, and he had the perfect plan.

After Arnold's first wife died, he married Peggy Shippen, a pretty young lady who came from a family who was loyal to King George. Peggy's family had connections in the British military, and one of Peggy's good friends was Major John André, an elite spy for the British Army. It was Peggy who introduced Arnold and André. Arnold decided that if America didn't want to act grateful for Arnold's work, he would become a spy for André and England. Plus, he could make more money as a spy, and Arnold liked money.

It was a terrible act of treason. Arnold was a friend of George Washington. He knew military secrets and was trusted with battle plans.

In 1780, George Washington asked Arnold to lead a raid against the British while Washington met with the French commanders. Washington had no idea that his old friend was now an enemy spy. Arnold had no desire to attack the British Army. He was working for them! So he told Washington that he had reinjured his bad leg and doctors said he needed to rest.

Washington respected Arnold and wanted to recognize him for all of his past work, so he appointed Arnold to an important but physically less demanding post—naming Arnold as the new commander of West Point. It was exactly what Arnold had hoped.

West Point would be the perfect gift to present to the British. With Arnold as commander, he could tell the British exactly when to attack and then turn the whole facility over to the English. It would humiliate and demoralize Washington and all of the American rebels. It would also be an astounding victory for the British.

But just handing over West Point wasn't enough for Benedict Arnold. He wanted to turn over as many American spies as he could. He believed that would make him even more popular with British General Henry Clinton. Arnold wrote a

# Benedict's the Best?

Some historians believe that Benedict Arnold was one of the best generals in the Continental Army. **Arnold's leadership at the battle of Saratoga forced the British Army to surrender.** That victory helped persuade the French to join the war and help the colonists. And it was because of the French that the colonists won the war.

very sneaky letter to Washington asking for the general to give him the names of any spies working in the area. Arnold used the excuse that he wanted to hire them to help protect West Point.

Fortunately, Washington did not give any of the names of the spies to Arnold. If he had, Arnold certainly would have turned them in and Washington's spies would have been killed.

Arnold was disappointed that he could not hand over the identities of the spies to General Clinton, but he tried to make up for it by filling West Point with as many guns and as much ammunition as he could get.

Everything was working exactly as Arnold had planned. New supplies arrived at West Point. Repairs were made to the fortifications and the garrison was full of soldiers and ammunition. Arnold was ready to enact his revenge. He wrote a letter addressed to a Mr. John Anderson and arranged for a business meeting.

John Anderson was actually British Major John André. During the meeting, Arnold was to give André all of the details needed for the British to march into West Point and take over the entire fort. Arnold was to be paid 20,000 British pounds (about $1.3 million in today's money) and given the rank of Brigadier General in the British Army.

André arrived on a British ship named the *Vulture* carrying false papers that gave him permission to conduct business with General Arnold. The meeting went well and plans were all in place, but strong winds had cause the ship to move away from the shore. It would be too difficult to row André back to the boat, so André decided that he would need to return to British headquarters by land. Arnold provided a horse and an unsuspecting officer to accompany him back. John André hid the important documents in his socks and put his boots on over them.

André and his escort were stopped at a colonial checkpoint, and even though André was escorted by a man from General Arnold's unit, the guards were suspicious. They asked André to take off his boots. He did, and one guard thought his socks looked strange. The guard searched André and found the papers. Immediately André was taken in for questioning.

When he arrived, the commanding officer, Colonel James, was afraid a terrible mistake had been made. He recognized General Arnold's signature on the pass held by André. He was afraid the superior officer would be furious with him because his men had detained his friend. Colonel James sent word to Arnold about André and asked for verification of André's story.

At the same time, Major Benjamin Tallmadge heard about what was going on. As one of General Washington's spies, he knew who André was and, with Washington's approval, had André arrested.

Benedict Arnold's grand scheme had fallen apart, but because of Colonel James, he also had a warning. Arnold was able to escape to a British ship where he pledged to serve King George. He was rewarded for his efforts by being made Brigadier General and was given a smaller cash gift of 6,000 pounds (about $350,000). He went on to lead British troops on raids in Virginia and Connecticut. And after the war, he settled with his wife Peggy in London.

Because Arnold had been such a hero to so many people, the colonial rebels took the news of his treason very hard. His name became synonymous with the word "traitor." Political cartoons appeared in newspapers and children would even insult each other by shouting, "You're a Benedict Arnold."

Benedict Arnold's grand scheme had fallen apart, but because of Colonel James, he also had a warning.

## Housewife Spy

Some spies are hired by the army and work for months or years at a time, but some spies are just regular people who just happen to be in the right place to learn critical information.

That was the case with Lydia Darragh. She was in the right place to learn an important piece of information and had the wisdom to know what to do with it.

William and Lydia Darragh had come from Ireland in 1753 to live in the Quaker community in Philadelphia. As Quakers, they were pacifists and did not believe in war, but secretly, the Darraghs did support the patriot cause. Their oldest son, William, was such an ardent patriot that he broke with Quaker tradition and joined the rebel army.

In September of 1777, the British took over the city of Philadelphia, and British General William Howe moved into the house across the street from the Darraghs. Lydia kept close watch on the comings and goings at the general's house and used her 14-year-old son to send messages about the general to her son in the army.

One day, the British knocked on the Darraghs' door and demanded that they let them use the house for a meeting place. Lydia was told that her family could remain in the house if she made sure that they all went to bed by eight o'clock in the evening and that no one should get up for any reason.

Of course, this made Lydia suspicious, but she followed orders and made sure her family was in bed at the early hour. But Lydia stayed awake, listening to the people arriving and chatter downstairs. She was sure it was an important meeting and decided that she needed to find out what was going on.

Lydia silently snuck out of her bedroom and went to a chamber room next to the room where the men were meeting. She overheard plans for an attack on Washington's troops stationed at Whitemarsh. The British were to strike in just 2 days.

Lydia crept back to her room and climbed into bed. A few minutes later, there was banging on her bedroom door. Lydia didn't get up. She pretended to be asleep. The pounding grew louder. She crawled out of bed and answered the door. A British soldier stood there and apologized for waking her. He told her the meeting was over, and they were leaving the Darraghs' house.

Lydia spent the rest of the night trying to figure out how to get the information to General Washington. She didn't want to tell any of her children or her husband. She didn't want them to be in danger of being caught as spies. Finally, she thought of a plan.

In the morning, she told her husband that the household was in need of flour. It was not an unusual errand for her to run, but she did go without her housemaid to help. Lydia had to get a pass from the British guards to go to the mill to get the flour. Once she filled her bag at the mill, she picked up her 25-pound bag of flour and walked for several more miles. She planned to go all the way to a pub in the neighboring town that was known to be a message center for patriots. Fortunately, she didn't have to hike all the way there.

As she was walking, she met a colonial officer she knew and told him what she had learned. The officer promised to deliver the message, and Lydia made the long hike back home with her bag of flour. Nobody suspected she had been delivering a spy's message.

General William Howe and his troops marched out to fight right on schedule. They were shocked to find General Washington and his troops armed and ready to fight. Who could have told them?

After 4 days of fighting, the battle was declared a standoff and Howe march his troops back to Philadelphia.

Howe was determined to find out who had told General Washington about his battle plans. An investigation was held and Lydia Darragh and her whole family were questioned. When it was Lydia's turn, the officer asked her if any of her family members had gotten out of bed. Lydia truthfully told him no. She was quite relieved that the officer never asked if *she* had gotten out of bed because she didn't want to have to lie.

Lydia Darragh was a housewife-turned-spy, and General Howe never knew it was her.

## Undercover Teacher

The British had their own set of spies working for them. **Ann Bates was a schoolteacher who volunteered to spy for King George.** She pretended to be a peddler selling thread, needles, and knives to the colonial camps. The whole time, she was spying on General Washington's troops and sending the information to the British.

# The Woman Called Wahatchee

The Cherokee Indians called her Wahatchee or "war woman." She stood 6 feet tall with flaming red hair and a face that was covered in freckles and smallpox scars. She wasn't pretty, but she was strong, an excellent hunter, and a crack shot.

Nancy Morgan Hart and her husband Benjamin lived in the Broad River Settlement of Georgia. They planted a huge apple orchard, and Nancy raised herbs that she used to doctor the people of the settlement. They loved their land and had strong patriot beliefs. Nancy was especially determined to do anything she could to help the American rebels gain their freedom from the rule of England. She even volunteered to act as a spy for the Georgia Whigs (rebels).

Nancy dressed as a man and acted like she was mentally unstable. Wandering around the camp, she was able to

# Homegrown Heroes

**Mary Draper** served the fight for colonial freedom by baking bread and melting pewter. As the call for troops went out in Connecticut, Mary Draper put her daughter and her maids to work baking enough bread to feed an army. **She set the bread out on boards in front of her house and gave it to the soldiers as they marched by.** When General Washington spread the word that ammunition was scarce, she melted down her own pewter cups and plates to make musket balls.

overhear the British plans. Nancy wandered back out of the camp and immediately gave the information to General Elijah Clarke.

When General Clarke needed information about an enemy camp in South Carolina, it was Nancy who made a crude raft from logs and grapevines, then crossed the Savannah River. She found out what the general wanted to hear and rowed her raft back across to give Clarke the information he needed.

After a while, the British began to suspect that Nancy was spying for the rebels and they sent someone to spy on her. One evening, Nancy was working inside her cabin when one of her children whispered that an eyeball was peering through a chink in the cabin wall. Nancy took a ladle full of hot water from the pot on the fire and threw it at the eyeball.

The spy screamed in pain. As he writhed on the ground, Nancy and her children tied him up and then delivered him as a prisoner to the local militia.

Nancy was always ready to help any patriot, and her friends and neighbors knew that. When one local patriot was being chased by British soldiers, he ran into Nancy's cabin. She sent him out the back and promised to get rid of the men chasing him.

Within a few minutes, a group of soldiers arrived at her door and demanded information. She calmly replied that no one had been near the cabin all day. The soldiers didn't believe her. One of them even shot her prize hen, then demanded she cook it for them. Nancy invited them in and opened up her supply of wine. Once the men were feeling the effects of the alcohol, she made a grab for their guns and managed to hold them all hostage until her husband arrived with help.

There are many more stories about Nancy and her bravery, but not all of them can be confirmed. What is true is that Nancy was a real patriot and a hero of the American Revolution. Hart County in Georgia was named after her and in 1997, she was inducted into the rolls of the Georgia Women of Achievement.

A replica of her log home, with chimney stones from the original cabin, is in the Nancy Hart Park in Elbert County, Georgia.

# Slave Turned Spy
## James Armistead Lafayette

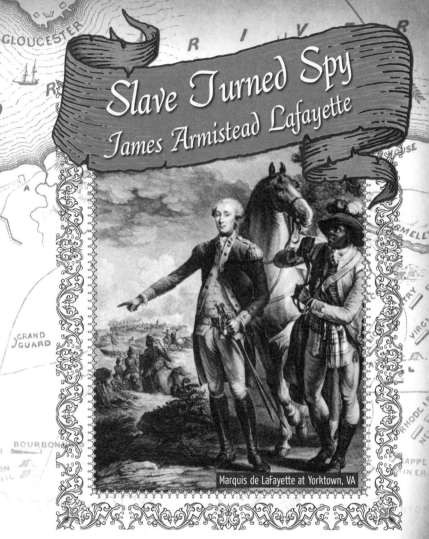

Marquis de LaFayette at Yorktown, VA

A man in tattered clothes wandered through the British army camp. Scruffy and dirty, he looked like one of the many escaped slaves who were searching for work and food. The camp commander definitely needed workers to help care for the horses, cook the food, and wash the clothing.

But this was no ordinary slave. This man was James Armistead, and he was a spy sent by the General Marquis de Lafayette, commander of the French forces allied with the colonists, to spy on the American traitor General Benedict

Eventually Armistead was able to pretend he was willing to spy for General Arnold. He promised to visit the colonial army and bring back information on what the American rebels were planning.

Arnold. After Arnold failed in his attempt to turn West Point over to the British, he went to work leading British troops in fights against the American rebels. It was up to James Armistead to find out how to stop him.

Unlike most slaves of the time, Armistead had been given an education by his master William Armistead. He knew how to read and write and was able to send detailed messages back to General Lafayette. The officers in Benedict Arnold's camp had no idea that the man who was serving them food and cleaning their uniforms was actually memorizing their battle plans and then sending those plans on to the Continental Army.

Armistead became so trusted by the British soldiers that General Arnold even asked him to act as a guide and lead the soldiers through unfamiliar territory. Eventually Armistead was able to pretend he was willing to spy for General Arnold. He promised to visit the colonial army and bring back information on what the American rebels were planning. This allowed Armistead greater mobility so that he could freely move from one camp to another. All the while, he was taking valuable information from the British and giving the British fake information from the rebels.

Always listening and paying attention to every detail, Armistead heard that British General Charles Cornwallis was moving his troops to Yorktown. This was critical information. Armistead immediately got word to Lafayette and the American rebels met a very surprised Cornwallis at Yorktown.

The battle that came next was fierce, but the rebels forced Cornwallis and his men to retreat to a peninsula where they were trapped. The British commander surrendered. Armistead had played a major role in helping the colonial rebels win the war.

After the war, General Lafayette returned to France and Armistead went back to work as a slave on his master's plantation. Three years later, Lafayette came back for a visit and was appalled to see that his old friend had not been freed. Lafayette wrote a letter to the Virginia state leaders telling them of the important work Armistead had done in the war.

With that certificate, Armistead was able to successfully petition the Virginia government to award him his freedom. He became a free man on New Year's Day, 1787. As a free man, he took the last name of Lafayette in honor of his army commander. James Armistead Lafayette purchased a farm in Kent County, VA, and was eventually awarded a pension for his service in the Revolutionary War. He died August 9, 1830, at the age of 70.

## Pompey's Mission

**Pompey Lamb was a slave** who worked as a deliveryman for the British, but he was actually a patriot spy. Trusted by the British, Pompey was given the code word to get into the fort at Stony Point, NY. **Pompey brought along two soldiers dressed as farmers.** The three men overpowered the guards and allowed the colonial rebels to capture the fort.

When Benjamin Franklin signed the Declaration of Independence on July 4, 1776, he was already 70 years old. He was famous in the colonies and Europe for his science experiments and the invention of the Franklin stove, bifocals, and the lightning rod. He was also well known for his essays and the publication of *Poor Richard's Almanack*. He could have retired and let the younger generation fight the battle for independence, but Franklin was a true patriot. He strongly believed that the colonies should govern themselves, and Franklin was willing to do anything to help, even act as a spy.

The colonies had no formal army or navy and very little in the way of supplies such as gunpowder. If they were to succeed in fighting the British Army, then they needed help from another country. Franklin had spent a great deal of time in Europe and had prominent friends in many countries. It was those connections that the colonies needed to help them in the war against the British.

Franklin started writing letters to his friends abroad. These letters had to be secret because if the King of England found out, Franklin and the people helping him could have been arrested or worse.

Franklin believed he had the best chance in getting help from France. The French had suffered an embarrassing defeat in the Seven Years' War. France was forced to surrender Canada and all of its land along the Mississippi River basin. All they had left were two small fishing islands off the south coast of Newfoundland. The French wanted vengeance on the British, and helping the colonists defeat the British army would be a sweet revenge.

But the French didn't want to be embarrassed again. They only wanted to help the American colonies if they were sure they could defeat Britain. So they were very cautious in their communication with Franklin.

Benjamin Franklin was known for being an excellent writer and used his skills to write convincing letters to officials in the French government. Eventually, the French sent their own intelligence officer to learn about the state of affairs in the colonies.

Disguised as a merchant from Antwerp, Julien Alexandre Achard de Bonvouloir arrived in Philadelphia and sought an introduction to the great Benjamin Franklin. Achard de Bonvouloir couldn't tell why he needed to see Franklin, just that he needed to talk to him in private.

Franklin agreed to meet with the young man, suspecting that he was an intelligence agent from France. They met in the upstairs rooms of the Library Company that had been founded by Franklin. They met at night when the building was empty and made sure the shutters were closed. Neither man wanted to be caught in a meeting that would be considered treason to the British.

# Father — Versus — Son

**Benjamin Franklin's son William was a loyalist and actually spied on his father.** He sent information about Benjamin Franklin to the British authorities. William was arrested by the colonists and held in prison. He eventually was exiled to Britain and never made up with his father.

Franklin was able to give the intelligence that was needed to convince Achard de Bonvouloir that it would be in France's best interests to help the colonies in the war. But the French government wasn't yet ready to help the colonists openly. They only agreed to help secretly with supplies and shipments of weapons.

Franklin and other members of the Continental Congress knew that they needed the French Army to help them if they had any hope of defeating the great British military. Congress appointed Franklin as its ambassador to France. In this official position, Franklin would have the ear of the people in the French government and he could convince them to send their army.

Franklin sailed for France on October 27, 1776. Once he was there, he used his charismatic personality to recruit people to become secret allies for the American cause. He sent secret messages back and forth, letting George Washington and the congress know the progress he was making. Ultimately Franklin was successful, and the French agreed to join the fight against the British. With the help of the French soldiers, the colonists won the war and France had its revenge on Britain.

# A Spy's Memory

Part of being a good spy is developing a good memory. Spies have to be very observant and then remember what they have seen. You can train your memory by giving it some exercise.

**Materials:**

- ❑ a partner
- ❑ a serving tray
- ❑ a bunch of random small items

- ❑ a towel
- ❑ a timer
- ❑ a pencil and paper

The items can be anything from toy cars, balls, or cards to silverware or toothpicks; any small item lying around your house will work.

While you wait in a separate room, have your partner take the serving tray and fill it with random small items. He or she should try to put at least 20 different items on the tray, then cover the tray with the towel. Return to the room. Have your partner place the tray in front of you and set the timer for one minute. Pull off the towel.

You will have one minute to look at the items on the tray. When the timer goes off, your partner should put the towel back over the tray and remove it from the room. You then have one minute to list all of the items that you saw on the tray. After your minute is up, check your answer with the actual items. How many did you get? You can increase your memory by practicing and adding more objects to the tray.

Good luck!

# Truth or Lie

Was that the truth
or is he lying?

Spies have to become very good at knowing if someone is telling the truth or if they are lying. They also have to be good at fooling other people with their own "lies." This is a great game for young spies to practice their skills. You will need some friends to help you with this spy training activity.

## Materials

❑ 5 or 6 friends ❑ Paper and pencil

Have your friends sit in a circle and give each person a piece of paper and a pencil. Tell your friends they are to write three statements on the paper about themselves. Two of the statements should be true and one should be false. The objective is to get everyone to believe all three of your statements by making them as close to the truth as possible.

After each person has written three statements, go around the circle and have each person read the statements. Have everybody guess which statements are true and which is a lie. The best spy will be able to fool everybody and also guess which of the other statements are lies.

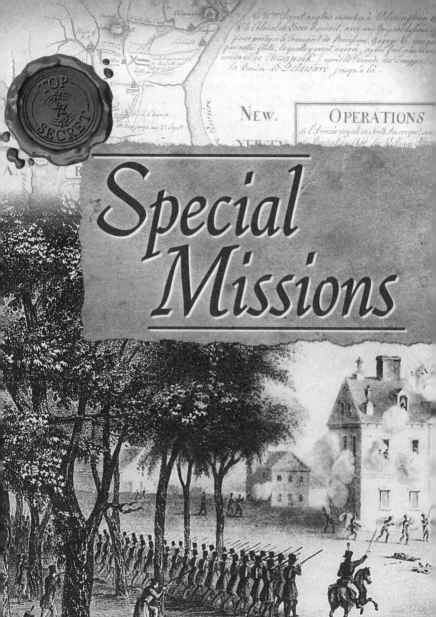

# Special Missions

# John Paul Jones's Raid

The moon glowed and the ropes creaked as the sailors lowered the two small boats into the Atlantic Ocean. Commander John Paul Jones directed the oarsmen to head for the port of Whitehaven, England. Their orders were to capture the British sailors and destroy their ships. It would be the first attack by Americans on British soil.

The men rowed quietly, their oars slicing through the dark water until they reached the shore. After they pulled the boat onto the land, they broke into two groups. John Paul Jones took 15 men and headed to the fort. Lieutenant Samuel Wallingford led the other men to the harbor to burn the ships.

Jones had his men hoist him over the wall of the fort. He dropped to the ground and waited to see if the sentry would sound the alarm. Silence was all Jones heard. The rest of his team climbed the wall and within a few minutes, they had captured the fort. The British soldiers were shocked by the attack and surrendered without a fight.

The Americans then spiked all of the guns by driving nails through the flame hole of the cannons so they couldn't fire. Jones marched all of the captured soldiers back to the boats and met Lieutenant Wallingford and his men. But Wallingford had failed in his mission. His candle had gone out. Matches had not yet been invented and lighting a fire with flint and steel took too long, so the common practice was to light a fire from one flame to another. Without the candle flame, they had no way to start a fire.

Jones made a daring move. While the captives were loaded on the ship, he sent a raiding party into town to steal some fire from a local tavern. They set

# "I Have Not Yet Begun to FIGHT"

As commander of the *Bonhomme Richard*, John Paul Jones fought in a terrible battle against the 44-gun Royal Navy frigate *Serapis*. Jones's own ship was burning and sinking, and he still refused the British demand for surrender. He yelled, "I have not yet begun to fight." Three hours later, it was the *Serapis* that surrendered and Jones took command.

a coal ship on fire and headed out of port. The townspeople rushed to the harbor and put out the fire on the ship but they couldn't fire on Jones's ship because all of the guns were spiked.

From Whitehaven, Jones and the crew sailed for St. Mary's Isle. Their mission—to kidnap the Earl of Selkirk. Jones was sure he could exchange the earl for American prisoners of war. Unfortunately, the raiding party found out that the earl wasn't at home. They had to settle for stealing the family's set of silver.

Disappointed, but still looking for victory for the American rebels, Jones and his men set sail across the Irish Sea. There they found the 20-gun sloop-of-war HMS *Drake*. It was a fierce battle with losses on both sides, but Jones managed to capture the *Drake*. It was the first time the Continental Navy had captured a British warship.

Jones and his crew were hailed as heroes, and Jones was later awarded the command of a 42-gun warship that he named *Bonhomme Richard* in honor of Benjamin Franklin.

Captain John Paul Jones

# Daring Dicey

Dicey Langston was a teenage girl with a mission. She was determined to help her older brothers in their fight for American freedom. Her brothers had all volunteered to fight for the rebel cause, and Dicey was willing to do anything to help them.

Living in South Carolina, many of the Langston neighbors were loyal to King George, so the brothers wisely decided to take their small band of patriot soldiers and camp several miles from the family plantation. They hoped that this would protect Dicey and their elderly father from acts of revenge from their loyalist neighbors. But the brothers hadn't counted on Dicey and her talent for spying.

At 15, Dicey was outgoing and friendly. She was an expert horse rider and an excellent shot. Dicey often visited neighbors and friends and overheard plans for troop movements. She stored the information in her memory and then made trips to the encampment where she shared the intelligence with her brothers and their patriot friends.

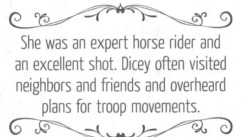

She was an expert horse rider and an excellent shot. Dicey often visited neighbors and friends and overheard plans for troop movements.

The loyalists began to be suspicious when the patriots seemed to know their every move. Soldiers visited Solomon Langston and accused him of being a spy. He denied knowing anything. The soldiers told him that if it was Dicey doing the spying, they would hold him accountable for her actions. He needed to keep better control of his daughter.

Worried about what might happen to his only daughter if she were caught, Mr. Langston banned her from visiting her brothers. Dicey knew it was important to her father and did stay away from camp for a while.

But when a group called the Bloody Scouts came to their neighborhood looking for her brothers and their friends, Dicey knew she had to do something. The Bloody Scouts were a band of English outlaws who were known for torturing and killing their victims. Dicey had to warn her brothers, even if it was against her father's orders.

That night, Dicey went on her most daring adventure. She snuck out of the house and began the 10-mile walk to her brother's camp. To avoid being seen, she stayed off the roads and ran through the woods and fields.

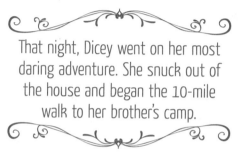

That night, Dicey went on her most daring adventure. She snuck out of the house and began the 10-mile walk to her brother's camp.

When she reached the Enoree River, she found that it was swollen with early spring floodwaters. The current was swift and the water was deep. It would be a dangerous crossing, but Dicey had no choice. She hiked up her skirts and petticoats and plunged into the river.

The current was strong and the swirling waters pulled her under twice. Dicey fought the river and pulled herself dripping and cold onto the opposite riverbank. After resting a few minutes, she got up and walked the rest of the way to the camp.

She arrived just a little after her brothers and their men returned from an expedition. The men were exhausted but grateful and agreed to leave the base. Dicey began the long walk back home. She made it back in time to cook her father breakfast. The old man never realized his daughter had been gone all night or that she had broken his rule about visiting her brothers.

It was all worth it, because when the Bloody Scouts attacked the camp, they found it completely deserted. The Bloody Scouts were furious and suspected Dicey and her father, but they had no way to prove it.

# Kate's Warning Ride

**The British were coming,** and Brigadier General Daniel Morgan needed help. Kate Barry was a young woman who knew the woods and back trails of her South Carolina home better than any soldier. When General Morgan asked for help, **Kate saddled her horse and rode through the countryside** telling the men to get ready to fight. With her help, General Morgan and his men were able to defeat Cornwallis and drive the British out of the state.

The Bloody Scouts decided they needed to teach the Langstons a lesson. They broke into the house, grabbed Dicey's father, and pointed a pistol at his chest. They accused him of being a traitor to the king and threatened to kill him.

Dicey was furious. She ran to her father and threw herself in between him and the gunman. She shouted at the Bloody Scouts, telling them to leave her father alone. Miraculously, they left without hurting Dicey or her father.

Dicey continued to spy on the loyalists and carry messages throughout the war. She was stopped by guards several times and once was threatened with being shot, but she never backed down. Her friends called her Daring Dicey.

After the colonists won the war, Dicey married Thomas Langston, a local patriot leader. She had 22 children and lived to be 71. Her obituary says that she left about 140 grandchildren and great-grandchildren. A marker was placed at her grave by the Daughters of the American Revolution and a school in South Carolina is name after her.

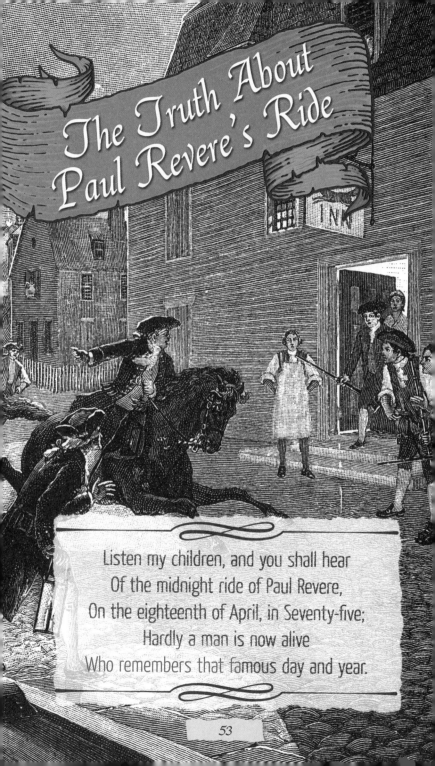

# The Truth About Paul Revere's Ride

Listen my children, and you shall hear
Of the midnight ride of Paul Revere,
On the eighteenth of April, in Seventy-five;
Hardly a man is now alive
Who remembers that famous day and year.

Many people have read Henry Wadsworth Longfellow's famous poem about Paul Revere's ride (part of which is included on the previous page), but most people don't know the truth about that leg-

> To read the complete Longfellow poem about Paul Revere's "midnight ride," go to this website: http://www.poetryfoundation.org/poem/173903

endary night: Paul Revere never actually finished his ride. And most people have no idea that Paul Revere was a rebel spy.

The truth is, on that night Paul Revere was captured by the British. Oh, and he didn't make the ride alone. He had a partner named William Dawes who was never mentioned in the poem, probably because his name didn't rhyme with year.

The famous poem about Paul Revere was published in 1860, nearly 100 years after the American Revolution. Longfellow never meant the poem to be taken as fact. It was a poem he wrote to remind people about the Americans who had worked so hard to build the United States of America. It was based on the truth, but was not factual. The truth was even more exciting than the poem.

Paul Revere was a member of the Sons of Liberty. It was an organization that started long before the American Revolution and was dedicated to the idea of helping the colonists be free from the taxes and rules imposed on them by the King of England. Other members of the Sons of Liberty were people like Samuel Adams, John Hancock, and John Adams.

During the time of the American Revolution, there were many people living in the colonies who were loyal to King George. They were called loyalists. The men who belonged to the Sons of Liberty were considered rebels because they rebelled against the laws of England. It was important that the rebels have spies who could learn about the orders coming from England and the plans of the British Redcoats. Paul Revere was just the person to work as a rebel spy.

Revere was a well-known silversmith working in Boston. He made silver items for both the British loyalists and colonists. Nobody would ever think it was suspicious for Revere to travel from Boston to other cities. He was a businessman who had to travel for his work.

It was true that Revere needed to travel for his work, but while he was traveling he was also collecting information about British Army movements. He would carry messages back and forth from one group of colonial rebels to another.

The British suspected that he was carrying messages and spying, but they never had enough proof to stop him. Revere was a popular figure in the colonies. If they accused him without proof, the colonists would be angry and might riot. The British wanted to keep things calm so they left Revere alone. That is, until the night of April 18, 1775.

That night, Paul Revere and William Dawes were watching for a signal from the belfry of the Old North Church in Boston. Rumor was, British military troops were coming to arrest some of the Sons of Liberty for acts of treason against

# Paul Revere, Dentist

One of Paul Revere's jobs was a dentist. **He used his skills as a silversmith to wire together dentures** that were made of walrus ivory or animal teeth. He was also the first person to practice forensic dentistry when he identified the body of his friend Joseph Warren by recognizing the wiring he had used to put in a false tooth.

the king. The British were going to take away the colonists' guns and weapons and seize their stores of gunpowder. It would leave the colonists defenseless. But if the colonists could be warned that the British soldiers were coming, then they could fight and defend themselves.

Revere arranged with his friend, Robert Newman, the sextant of Old North Church in Boston, to give a signal to the people of Charlestown. One lantern meant the British would be moving by land south of town, and two lanterns meant they were crossing the river north of town. The signal was not for Revere, but meant to warn the citizens if the riders could not get through with the message.

That night, Paul Revere received information from other spies that the British were indeed planning to capture and imprison John Hancock and Samuel Adams and attack the colonists. So Dawes and Revere each took off in different directions. They would ride out and warn the people in the

## The British Are Coming!
### (Or Are They?)

Paul Revere never shouted the legendary phrase "The British are coming!" **The warning was done quietly** by knocking on doors and secretly letting people know that they needed to be ready to fight. Also at that time, the colonists considered themselves to be British and the British Army was called the Regulars. **So the warning was, "The Regulars are coming."**

countryside. There, more riders would take up the call and ride on farther until the whole countryside as far as Concord, MA, would be warned and ready to fight. By the end of the night, there were nearly 40 riders helping to warn the colonists.

It was a good thing that Paul Revere and William Dawes were not the only riders, because if they were, then it would have been a disaster. Revere and Dawes made their rides through the countryside and met in Lexington at the house where Adams and Hancock were staying. After warning their friends, the riders took off for Concord, but only made it as far as a British checkpoint outside of Lexington.

Dawes and another rider managed to escape, but Paul Revere was held and questioned. Revere pretended to cooperate and told the British there were thousands of colonists ready to fight. Of course it was all a bluff, but when the British soldiers heard gunshots in Lexington and the church bells ringing, the soldiers got scared and ran off to find their regiment. They left Paul Revere and stole his horse. Revere walked back into town to the house where John Hancock and Samuel Adams were staying. Revere then helped Hancock and his family escape with their belongings, including a trunk full of important documents about plans for the proposed government of the United States.

If not for the work of Paul Revere, the spy, America would have lost two of its most important patriot leaders and most of its guns and ammunition. Without Revere's work, the American Revolution could have had a very different ending.

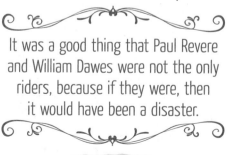

It was a good thing that Paul Revere
and William Dawes were not the only
riders, because if they were, then
it would have been a disaster.

# Molly Pitcher

Generals in the modern U.S. Army would never put up with families following their soldier to the battlefield, but that's exactly what General Washington had to deal with. In the American Revolution, it was common practice to have numerous people who traveled with the army as camp followers. They were family members, often wives, who went with their husbands to war. The women and older children helped by working as cooks, nurses, and servants for the soldiers. They cared for the soldiers who were sick or wounded, carried messages, mended uniforms, and washed clothes. They also carried pitchers of water out to the soldiers as they were drilling or when they were in battle.

Mary Ludwig Hays was a camp follower. In 1777, she went to war with her husband, William Hays and spent the winter with General Washington and his troops at Valley Forge. Mary's nickname, like many women of the time, was Molly.

One of Molly's jobs was to carry pitchers of water to the soldiers firing the cannons. The water was used to cool down the hot cannon barrel. It was also used by the soldier working the ramrod. The ramrod was a long pole that had a sponge on the end of it. It had two purposes. First it was shoved into the mouth of the cannon to tightly pack the cannonballs against the gunpowder. And after the cannon was fired, it was used to clean the sparks and gunpowder out of the cannon barrel. The men called for Molly and her pitcher of water so often that her nickname became Molly Pitcher.

In June of 1778, Molly and her husband were fighting at the Battle of Monmouth in New Jersey. It was a sweltering day

## Mrs. Washington Goes to War

Martha Washington was one of the most famous camp followers. **Every winter for 8 years of the revolution, she joined her husband wherever he was stationed.** She wasn't the only camp follower, however: It is estimated that there were 11,000 soldiers camped at Valley Forge and 400 camp followers helped attend to their needs.

with temperatures over 100 degrees. It was even hotter firing the blazing hot cannons. The soldiers kept yelling for Molly to bring more pitchers. She ran back and forth from the spring to keep the soldiers supplied.

The next time she ran to the cannon, she found that her husband had collapsed and had to be carried off the battlefield. That left the cannon crew short a person. Molly grabbed the ramrod and took over pounding the gunpowder and cannonballs into the gun barrel.

Cannons fired back at them and shots whistled through the air, but Molly kept at her post, using her husband's ramrod the entire battle.

To give herself leverage, Molly stood with her feet spread apart as far as her long skirts would allow. It was a good thing too, because at one point, an enemy cannonball flew between her legs and ripped away her petticoats. Molly just ignored the cannonball and her missing skirt and kept working.

Molly's work paid off. The battle was a major victory for the Continental Army and the British forces retreated during the night. After the battle, General Washington asked his aides who was the woman loading the cannons. He was so impressed with Molly's courage that he issued her a warrant as a noncommissioned officer. For the rest of her life, Molly was known as "Sergeant" Molly.

# Knowlton's Rangers

Thomas Knowlton joined the army when he was just 15. His older brother, Daniel, went off to fight in the French and Indian War, and, amazingly, Thomas's parents said he could go along. Daniel was an experienced scout and instructed Thomas in practical skills, such as how to follow a trail, how to camouflage himself in the woods, and how to track an enemy. These were talents that Thomas certainly needed.

As a teenager, he found himself fighting against both skilled Indian warriors and trained French soldiers. In one battle, he was surrounded by Indian fighters. He fired shots and scrambled through brush, escaping only to find himself in the middle of group of French soldiers. Thomas managed to sneak off without being caught and found his way back to his own fighting unit.

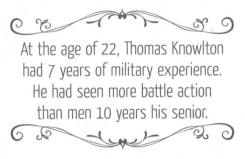

At the age of 22, Thomas Knowlton
had 7 years of military experience.
He had seen more battle action
than men 10 years his senior.

Thomas was an excellent student and a crack shot. He learned his tracking lessons so well that by the time the war ended, he had been promoted to the rank of lieutenant and was leading his own scouting missions.

When military leader Israel Putnam needed men to go fight in the battle of Havana, Cuba, Thomas volunteered. His ship sailed for the tropical island in 1762. There Thomas and his fellow soldiers fought a vicious and bloody battle against the Spanish army. They captured Havana but at heavy cost of life. After the battle was won, the soldiers had a new enemy: disease. Twice as many soldiers died from tropical diseases as the number who had been killed in battle. Thomas was one of the lucky ones. He survived both the battle and the illness. Out of the 107 men who sailed off to battle with Israel Putnam, only 20 returned. Thomas was one.

At the age of 22, Thomas Knowlton had 7 years of military experience. He had seen more battle action than men 10 years his senior. When he returned home to Connecticut, he decided it was time to settle down. He married Anna Keys and they raised nine children.

But when the American colonists started their war of independence, Thomas was ready to fight for his country. As captain of the Ashford Company militia, Thomas led his men to the fight of Bunker Hill. His troops provided cover fire for the colonists as they retreated from the battle. His men were credited with saving countless colonists' lives. For his brave leadership, he was promoted to major.

George Washington then called upon Thomas for some very special help. Washington knew of Thomas's history as a skilled scout. He asked Thomas to train a select group of young men and prepare them to be able to fight in the woods and act as scouts. Washington wanted Thomas to lead a group of soldiers who could be trusted with special missions and secret operations. These men were given the name Knowlton's Rangers. For leading this elite fighting group, Thomas was promoted to the rank of lieutenant colonel. One of the members of Knowlton's rangers was Captain Nathan Hale.

The Rangers were assigned to the most hazardous duties. They were expected to scout deep in enemy territory and provide intelligence to Washington's headquarters. They were always to be ahead of Washington's army so that the main army would not be caught in a surprise attack. They were called upon to sacrifice their lives so that the larger army would be protected.

The rangers did exactly that. On September 16, 1776, Knowlton's Rangers were scouting in advance of Washington's army in New York when they discovered the Black Watch. It was a group of elite Highlander British fighters, and they were waiting for Washington's men. Knowlton's Rangers did what they had been trained to do. They fought bravely and protected the larger army from the Black Watch.

During the battle, Thomas was killed, but the rangers were successful in protecting Washington's army from a disastrous surprise attack. Washington was dismayed at Thomas's death and declared that "The brave and gallant Colonel Knowlton was an honor to any country."

Today the United States Army Rangers trace their roots back to the formation of Knowlton's Rangers. Like Knowlton's Rangers, today's Army Rangers are specially trained to be elite fighting forces. They conduct special missions and are known for their special ability to remain undetected. Their motto is "Rangers lead the way."

SPY TRAINING

# Target Practice

Spies and secret agents always need to be ready to defend themselves. Military spies have target practice on a regular basis, and you need target practice, too. Your target practice will not use anything as dangerous as musket or cannonballs, instead you will use cotton swabs and drinking straws.

## Materials

- ❏ Package of cotton swabs
- ❏ Drinking straws
- ❏ A paper target, made from poster board
- ❏ Masking tape

You will practice launching a projectile at a target. The projectiles are the cotton swabs and your launcher is the straw. Place a cotton swab in the straw and blow it toward your target.

You can draw your own paper target using poster board or use one that is premade. Place the target on the ground. Six to eight feet from the target, lay a strip of masking tape on the floor. This marks your launch line. You cannot step over this line when you launch your projectiles. Stand behind the line and practice your target shooting.

## War

Once you are proficient at hitting a target, it is time to practice your fighting techniques. You can have a cotton swab war with one friend or several, using your launchers from the target practice and a timer.

Divide your room or space in half and place a masking tape line down the middle. Divide into two equal teams. Give each team member a straw and an equal number of cotton swabs. Set the timer for 3 minutes.

Start the timer and have everyone fire the cotton swabs at the opposite side of the line. When the time is up, the winner is the side that has the least number of cotton swabs.

# Rule of Thumb

Your mission is to spy on the enemy's weapons. How many are there? How big? How wide? How tall? Of course you can't just pull out a measuring tape—that would be suspicious! So what do you do? You use the old fashioned rule of thumb. It's exactly what spies in the American Revolution used to take measurements, and it's as easy as looking at your thumb.

For centuries, people used body parts as forms of measurement. The English measurement of a "foot" or 12 inches originally came from the standard size of a man's foot. You can measure the length of a room by stepping off the number of feet it is from one wall to another.

An inch was originally the width of a man's thumb and a cubit was the distance from a man's elbow to his fingertips. For a long distance, you measure it in paces. A pace is two steps and a mile is a thousand paces.

As a spy, you need to be able to estimate sizes and distance without attracting attention. If you know the rules of ancient measuring systems, then you can make a good estimate of distance without any tools except your body. The "rules of thumb" are:

➢ inch = the width of the thumb.

➢ digit = the width of the middle finger (about 3/4 inch)

➢ palm = the width of four fingers (about 3 inches)

➢ span = the distance covered by the spread hand (about 9 inches)

➢ foot = the length of the foot (about 12 inches)

➢ cubit = distance from the elbow to the tip of the middle finger (about 18 inches)

➢ yard = distance from the center of the body to the fingertips of the outstretched arm (about 36 inches)

➢ fathom = distance spanned by the outstretched arms (about 72 inches)

Test your spy knowledge by measuring your bedroom.
After you record your estimates, you can use a
measuring tape to check how close you are.
How long is your room? _____
How many feet? _____
How many yards? _____

Now measure your schoolbooks.
How many inches? _____
How many digits? _____

You can see how learning to measure with your body
parts is an excellent tool for a spy. You can estimate
size without making anyone suspicious and quickly get
important statistics.

# The Measure of Man

Leonardo da Vinci recognized that
the human body's proportions
were a great tool for
measurement. His famous
drawing "Vitruvian Man"
explained proportions to
the people of the Middle
Ages. These measurements
were still in use during
the American Revolution.

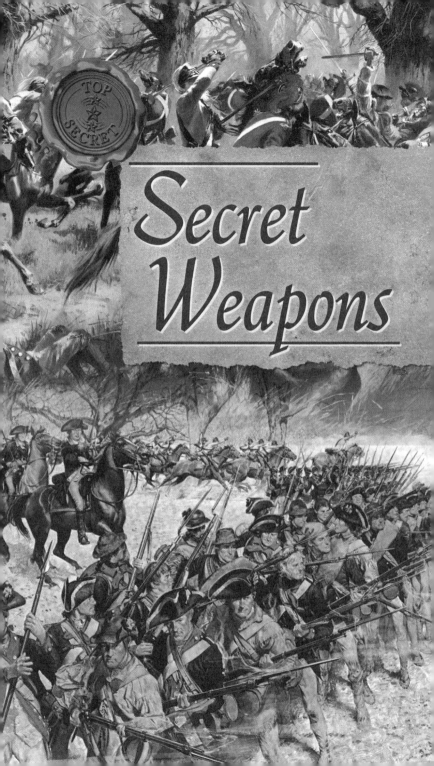

# Secret Weapons

# Brown Bess

Brown Bess was a soldier's best friend during the American Revolution. Bess was the British nickname for a muzzle-loading flintlock musket. The nickname probably came from the German words "braun buss," which mean "strong gun."

Brown Bess was also referred to as a long gun because, well, it was long! A Brown Bess stood 58 1/2 inches tall. That's as tall as an average fifth-grade boy. It weighed 10.5 pounds and had a bayonet attached to the barrel of the gun.

The gun was an improvement over old-fashioned match-lock guns that required the soldier to actually light a match to ignite the gunpowder and make the fire. Brown Bess used flint striking against steel to cause a spark that would set off the gunpowder. The biggest problem with the flintlock was that it didn't work very well in rainy weather. So if it was raining, there usually weren't any battles.

Brown Bess was also one of the first "pattern guns." This means that the guns were all developed from one pattern and made exactly alike. Before pattern guns were invented, gun owners would order their individual weapon from a gunsmith and no two guns were the same. If something broke on the gun, you could not buy a replacement part. It would have to be made special by the gunsmith. Pattern guns had all the same parts. This was really important for armies because they could keep spare parts on hand. If a gun part broke, then it could be replaced without taking it to a gunsmith.

Another problem with Brown Bess was that she was only accurate if the shot was less than 100 yards from the target. And in reality, it was best if the target was only 50 to 75 yards away.

## The First Bayonets

**Bayonets were first used in the 1600s by hunters in France and Spain.** They attached knives to the end of their muskets when they were hunting wild boar and dangerous game. Before the invention of the bayonet, soldiers had to have pikemen defend the musketeers from being attacked while they were reloading.

The Ferguson Ordnance Rifle was used by the British Army in the American Revolutionary War at the end of the 1770s

Because of this, the British designed a specific way to fight. The armies fought in groups of men called regiments. The regiments would line up face to face and fire two or three volleys. (A volley was when all of the men fired at once.) After they fired, they would charge and fight with their bayonets.

The American colonists were at a great disadvantage because most of them had never learned how to drill or march as a regiment. Plus, they didn't have as many weapons or enough gunpowder. At the start of the war, most men were using whatever weapons they had in their homes. A few states had stores of weapons for their militias, but, for the most part, the colonial rebels were greatly outgunned.

As the war progressed, the Continental Congress placed orders with American gunsmiths to make as many flintlocks as possible. The rebel soldiers also captured as many guns as they could from the British. The capture of a Brown Bess was considered a great prize and was immediately put to use by the new owner.

# The Turtle Submarine

General George Washington needed the New York Harbor. It was an important port for receiving supplies, arms, and munitions, but it was completely controlled by the British. Washington was looking for anything that could help them beat the British blockade.

Young David Bushnell had been working on underwater explosives since he was a student at Yale. After 5 years of experimenting, he had perfected a method for setting off a charge underwater. Next, he began working on a way to attach the explosive to an enemy ship without being seen. He designed a vehicle that could go under the water. It was a one-man, hand-cranked power submarine called the *Turtle* because it looked like a turtle shell.

For 2 years, Bushnell worked in secret perfecting the *Turtle*'s ability to dive and ascend. It was designed to be a one-man vessel and contained enough air for about 30 minutes of submersion. It could travel at the top hand-crank speed of 3 miles per hour. Bushnell saw to every detail and even tried to make the controls glow in the dark by using bioluminescent foxfire (a type of fungus that glows). But Bushnell found that when the foxfire got too cold, it would stop glowing. He wrote to Benjamin Franklin to ask for suggestions.

When Franklin heard about the submarine, he helped bring it to the attention of George Washington. Washington was not sure that the underwater vessel would work, but he agreed to give some money for Bushnell to continue his experiments.

In August of 1776, Bushnell decided that the *Turtle* was ready for a mission. General Washington ordered the *Turtle* to be hauled to the New York Harbor. Late at night on

The Drebbel submarine, 1620

## The First Submarine

The world's first submarine was actually built by Cornelius Drebbel in the 1620s. He crafted a wooden submarine powered by oarsmen who breathed through snorkel air tubes. He tested his craft in the waters of the Thames River and was able to submerge the boat 12 to 15 feet below the surface, but the British Navy never actually used his invention.

The goal of the mission was huge. They were going to attack Admiral Richard Howe's flagship, the HMS *Eagle*.

September 6, 1776, the *Turtle* was launched into the harbor with Sergeant Ezra Lee at the controls. He had been trained by David Bushnell on how to drive the *Turtle* up close to a ship and then attach the explosive to the underside of the ship.

The goal of the mission was huge. They were going to attack Admiral Richard Howe's flagship, the HMS *Eagle*. Sergeant Lee spent nearly 2 hours cranking the *Turtle* through the dark waters. When he got close to the ship, he submerged and drove in close to the ship, but he could not get the explosive to attach to the ship.

According to Sergeant Lee, the British sent a rowboat out to investigate him. Lee decided it was best to release the explosive and hope it would ward off the curious British soldiers. The explosive floated out away from the ships and blew up, sending huge spouts of water into the air. Lee made it back to the shore. His trip had not been successful in bombing the HMS *Eagle*, but it was the first time a submarine had ever been used in battle.

In October, another attempt was made. This time the goal was a British frigate anchored off Manhattan, but that mission also failed. A few days later, the British attacked the ship that carried the *Turtle* and the submarine sank with the ship.

George Washington late wrote about the *Turtle* and its mission, saying it was "an effort of genius." It would be almost 100 years before there was a successful attack made by an underwater vessel.

# Innovative Artillerymen

During the American Revolution, artillerymen were considered elite forces. They were like the Green Berets or Special Ops forces of today. Why were they so special? Because they knew math.

In the 1700s, many people in both Britain and the American colonies were illiterate. There was no public school system, so most men and women could not read or do complex math calculations, and firing cannons required geometric calculations in order to get the cannonball to hit its intended target. Besides knowing how to do mathematical calculations, the artillery troops had to have a good understanding of the science of gunpowder and the physics of mortars. There were specific amounts of powder needed according to the size and weight of the shell that was being shot. The artillery troops were some of the smartest and best educated soldiers on the battlefield.

With such brainy guys working with the cannons, it's not surprising that they came up with some creative innovations for their guns and ammunition. One invention was called the "Galloper gun." It was a lightweight cannon that was mounted on a platform between two wagon wheels so that it could be pulled by a horse. Cannons were so heavy that they were usually mounted in one place and used only in that location. A lightweight cannon that could be moved was a revolution. Armies could haul their cannons to the place they needed to fight.

Cannons usually shot cannonballs. These were large metal balls that were projected into the air by an explosion of gunpowder. The smallest cannonballs were 2 pounds and the largest weighed 50 pounds. Artillery gunners also began to invent new projectiles to shoot out of the cannon barrel. They started using shells—hollow metal spheres. The shells were filled with loose metal and stones. As the shell traveled through the barrel, the friction caused the metal to explode and instead of one big cannonball, thousands of small projectiles flew through the air.

During the American Revolution, they used a canvas bag to hold lead and iron balls. The canvas bag was wrapped with twine to make it into a shape that would fit in the mouth of the cannon. With the twine tied around the bag, it looked like a bunch of grapes, so it was, of course, called grapeshot.

Grapeshot could travel for about 600 yards but not much farther. So it was effective only if the enemy was fairly close. It did provide a way to keep a buffer zone between the fighting troops.

Artillery soldiers also experimented with split shot, which consisted of two whole cannonballs connected by a length of chain. When the cannonballs were shot out of the muzzle, the cannonballs would fly in different directions until the chain pulled tight, and then it would rotate around its center of mass. It was especially effective in knocking down masts of ships.

Another invention was hot shot. The iron shot was heated in a red hot fire and then loaded into the cannon. This was incredibly dangerous for the artillery soldiers who had to load the fiery hot shot into the cannons, but it was effective when the soldiers were aiming at flammable targets, such as warships, buildings, or even gunpowder storage sheds.

All of these innovations came from artillerymen who knew their math and science well enough to be successful inventors.

# Chinese Firepower

**The Chinese invented gunpowder and the first guns.** At first they used hollow bamboo tubes packed with gunpowder, but soon they were experimenting with **gunpowder-filled bombs made from pottery or metal**. They even developed rapid-fire cannons like a seven-barrel cannon attached to a cart. **They were literally centuries ahead of the Europeans.**

# Dead Drops & Invisible Ink

The spy crossed the street, dodging carriage wheels and horse carts. He looked to one side and then the other. Was anyone watching? Had anyone followed him? He walked swiftly down the street past women in long skirts and shop-keepers hawking their wares. He didn't pause until he had reached the hardware shop. He reached into his jacket and pulled out a small piece of paper and dropped it in a metal bin next to the shop. Without looking back, the spy melted into the crowd of shoppers.

Within a few minutes, a different man walked up to the bin and pulled out the piece of paper. He grinned. He was sure he had finally located the colonial spy's dead drop. He unfolded the paper and found it was just a shopping list with all of the items checked off. He threw the paper down. Another waste of his valuable time.

Scenes like this played out during the American Revolution on both sides of the conflict. Spies had to get messages back and forth, and to protect the identity of their partners, they often left their messages in secret places called dead drops. This allowed the spies to leave and pick up messages without meeting face to face. Any place could be designated a dead drop. It could be as simple as a tree stump along a walking path or as complex as safebox hidden in a pub house. Just in case the dead drop was discovered by another agent, messages were often written in code or even in invisible ink, and sometimes both.

Invisible ink was not a new invention during the American Revolution. It had been in use for more than 2,000 years. The Ancient Greeks and Romans made invisible ink from the milk of the tithymalus plant. During the Renaissance, inventor Giovanni Battista Della Porta developed a recipe for invisible ink using an ounce of alum and a pint of vinegar. It worked by using the mixture to write on the shell of a hard-boiled egg. The liquid would seep through the shell and transfer the message onto the white of the egg. The message could only be read after carefully peeling the egg.

During the American Revolution, both sides used invisible inks. Any acid that will weaken the fibers of paper will work. When the weakened paper is held next to a heat source, it will darken or burn. Then all you have to do is read the message burned into the paper. Lemon juice or milk can both be used as inks.

The handy part about this type of invisible ink is that you can write a regular letter right over the message. When the spy is delivering the letter, it will look like a common everyday shopping list or a letter to a sweetheart. It's not until it is held next to a heat source that anyone will know that it contains a secret message.

George Washington wanted his agents to use the method of "sympathetic stain." This required that the letter writer have a special chemical compound to be used to write his letters and the recipient of the letter had a different chemical compound to brush onto the letter to make the writing appear. It was much more complex, but it was also much harder for enemy agents to find the invisible messages.

Dr. James Jay developed a special chemical mixture that George Washington provided to his agents. The mixture was expensive and time consuming to produce and often the agents were in short supply of the "white ink." When Washington needed more of the ink, he wrote to Dr. Jay and requested more "medicine."

Washington also advised his agents to use the ink to write on things such as almanacs or printed pamphlets, and he strongly believed in codes or encryption. Washington himself used at least four different cipher alphabets. Benjamin Franklin used a complicated diplomatic cipher that was developed by Charles William Frederick Dumas. It involved turning the 26-letter alphabet into a code of 682 numbers.

The British used a method called "masking." The spy would handwrite a regular letter and within that letter was a secret message. The message could be found when the reader placed a special "mask" over the letter. The mask was a separate sheet of paper with a shape cut out of it. When the mask was on top of the letter, the reader could find the words that were the message. The problem was that sometimes the reader never received the "mask," and they spent hours trying to find the message.

Another form of encryption used was the book code. The sender and receiver had to have the same version of a book. Often the spies used the dictionary or a Bible because many homes had these books. A code word would consist of a number that told the page of the dictionary, then a letter that told which paragraph, and then another number that told the word in the paragraph. It was a tedious way to write a code, but it was also difficult to decipher.

George Washington and his agents were considered masters at spycraft. After the war, British Major George Beckwith said, "Washington did not really outfight the British, he simply outspied us."

## Cabinet Noir

Reading other people's mail has always been a good way for spies to learn information. Spies in Europe had experts stationed in the post offices who were able to intercept mail, read it, copy passages for decoding, and then reseal it so that it looked like it had never been opened. They took on the name "black chamber" or *cabinet noir*, and nobody's mail was safe, not even the king's.

# Message Eggs

You can send a secret message inside a hard-boiled egg just like a spy. All you need are some simple household supplies.

## Materials

- ❑ Hard-boiled eggs
- ❑ 1 tablespoon alum (check the spice section of your grocery store for alum powder)
- ❑ 2 cups white vinegar
- ❑ Fine-tipped toothbrush or a toothpick
- ❑ High-intensity light (200 watts)

Dissolve the alum in the vinegar. Stir it until all of the alum is dissolved.

*Watertown Tavern, May 25, 1775 11 o'clock*

Dip your brush or toothpick into the solution and write your message on the shell of the egg. Then place the egg under the light for 10 minutes. The heat of the light will help the alum be darker on the egg.

The writing will be visible when you peel the shell off the egg!

# Invisible Ink

Every spy needs a good recipe for making his or her own invisible ink. Here are two tried and true recipes that will help you in writing all of your secret messages.

**BAKING SODA INK**
**Materials**

- ❏ Baking soda
- ❏ Tablespoon
- ❏ Water
- ❏ Glass
- ❏ Cotton swab
- ❏ Paintbrush
- ❏ White paper
- ❏ Grape juice

Mix equal parts baking soda and water in the glass. A good starting point is one tablespoon of each. When it is thoroughly mixed, dip your cotton swab into the solution and use it to write a message on the white paper. Let your message dry completely.

When the letter is dry, you can expose the writing by painting it with grape juice.

## LEMON JUICE INK
## Materials
- ❏ White paper
- ❏ Two fresh lemons
- ❏ Glass
- ❏ Cotton swab
- ❏ Lightbulb

Squeeze the juice of two lemons into the glass. Use your cotton swab to write your secret message with the lemon juice. Let the paper dry completely. After it is dry, hold the paper next to a bright lightbulb. The heat from the light will make the message appear.

SPY TRAINING

# Spy Blocker

The biggest fear of a spy is getting caught—especially by another spy! You can protect yourself from invasion with a simple toothpick.

You don't need to make a fancy door alarm to know if anyone has been snooping through your room. Just take a toothpick and break it in half to make it smaller. Save the other half—you can use it later. Insert the piece of toothpick between your bedroom door and the door frame and gently close the door.

When you return to your room, look to see if the toothpick is still in the door. If it's not, then someone opened your door while you were gone!

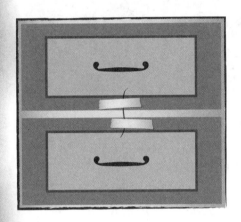

You can also set traps on your dresser or desk drawers. For this, you simply need some clear tape and a piece of thread. Cut a small piece of thread and use clear tape to attach it to your drawers. If anyone opens your drawers while you are gone, then the thread will be broken.

These are two great ways to tell if anyone is spying on you or if your siblings are trying to borrow your stuff without asking.

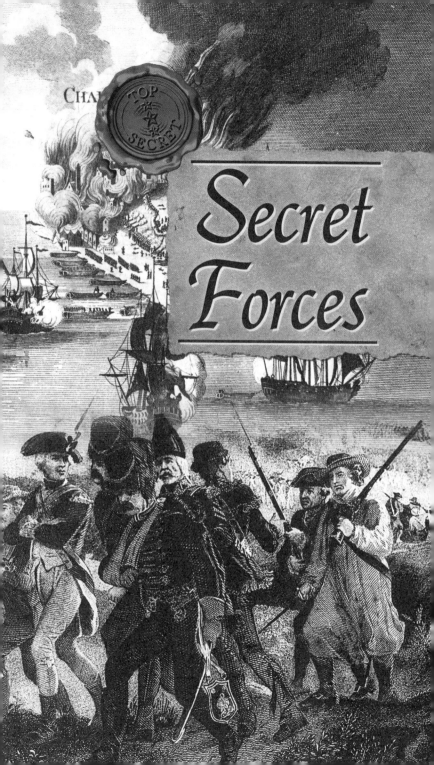

# Secret Forces

# Pirates of the Revolution

How do you fight a war when you don't have a navy? That was the problem General Washington had when the American Revolution started. For many years, the colonies had been protected by the British Navy. But in 1775, when the colonies went to war with Britain, they had no navy of their own and the British had the most powerful navy in the world. It was a problem. A very big problem.

At the start of the American Revolution, the British had 131 naval warships. The American colonies had none. Building a warship required time and money, neither of which the colonial rebels had. In June of 1776, British Admiral Richard Howe arrived in New York Harbor with a huge fleet of ships that carried 23,000 British soldiers and 9,000 hired German mercenaries. New Yorkers said the harbor had so many ship masts it looked like a forest.

It was a desperate situation. The British Navy easily blocked the New York Harbor and sent ships to try to block harbors up and down the East coast of the colonies. If the British were successful, they could block all goods coming in to the colonies, even desperately needed gunpowder and weapons.

George Washington did the only sensible thing: He authorized private citizens to become pirates and attack the British Navy.

During the 1700s and 1800s, governments could give ship owners documents called "letters of marque." These letters were written and signed by the leaders of a country and authorized private citizens to attack any vessels that were deemed enemies of their home country. If a ship's captain had a letter of marque from the American colonies, it meant the ship could attack a British ship and the crew would not be prosecuted as pirates. Without the letter, anyone who attacked a ship and looted it was considered a pirate and if caught could be prosecuted and executed.

Holding a letter of marque also meant that the ship's captain and crew could take all of the supplies on the ship and keep them for themselves as payment. They could even sell the ship and split the money. It was a huge incentive for colonial ship owners to attack British ships.

It was a brilliant plan. Piracy was a sure way to cause problems for the British. They had to watch out for every ship that didn't carry a British flag. And the colonists were quite happy to take the risk because often the rewards were huge.

Ordinary seamen earned $9 a month. A privateer could earn $1,000 a month. Men could go to sea and earn a fortune, or they could be killed. It was dangerous because the British ships had better weapons than the American colonists, but many men thought it was worth the risk.

During the war, thousands of men and boys worked as privateers. Some boys went to sea when they were only 13.

## Better Than Buried Treasure

**Records show that some privateers became quite wealthy from their dangerous work.** Records of the privateer ship *Hope* show that the prize for a 14-year-old cabin boy was as follows: $7,000, 1 ton of sugar, 35 gallons of rum, 20 pounds of cotton, 20 pounds of sugar, 20 pounds of ginger, 20 pounds of allspice, and 20 pounds of logwood. A normal year's wages would have been $144.

The privateers often used tricks to capture the ships. They would fly the flag of a different country to fool the British ship into thinking it was safe to go near them. Then they would sail alongside the ship and climb aboard with guns and rifles and capture the crew.

Next, they sailed the captured ship to the nearest friendly harbor where they could sell the goods and auction the ship. The British seamen were taken as prisoners. Of course, sometimes the British would get revenge and would recapture their own ships or they would sink the attacking privateers.

At the end of the war, the American colonies did build some ships and started a proper fighting navy, but the privateers had done the job Washington needed. They had successfully interfered with the British ships and helped end the blockades.

# Minutemen

They were listening for a knock on the door. Watching for a signal light. They had pledged to be ready at a minute's notice. To throw on their clothes, man their weapons, and be ready for battle within 30 minutes of getting the signal. They were the Minutemen. An elite group of fighting men who were specially trained to be first on the battlefield.

A Minuteman was to be 25 years old or younger and was chosen from the ranks of local militia for his enthusiasm, reliability, and physical strength. It was the Minutemen who were waiting for the signal from Paul Revere and William Dawes in April of 1775.

The Minutemen had been a part of the colonial military since the mid 1600s. The Minutemen were active in the French and Indian War in the 1750s, and by the time the American Revolution arrived, there had been six generations of Minutemen fighting in Massachusetts.

## Modern-Day Minuteman

The U.S. Air Force named the LGM-30 Intercontinental Missile the "Minuteman" because it was designed for rapid deployment in the event of a nuclear attack. The "Minuteman III" is still guarding the U.S. today, ready at a moment's notice.

The British were quite surprised by the fighting techniques of the Minutemen. The Redcoats fought in the traditional regimental formation with men marching and firing in rows of soldiers. The Minutemen had learned how to fight during the French and Indian War, and they used irregular warfare. They hid in trees and bushes and would act as sharpshooters. The guns used by the Minutemen were usually their own hunting rifles. These rifles were more accurate than the British muskets, but they took longer to load. The Minutemen employed the tactic of "shoot and scoot." They would take a shot, and then have to quickly change their location to reload.

It was a tactic that surprised the British. Officers in the Royal Armies were warned to take off their brass medals and emblems because sharpshooting Minutemen would aim for the men in gold. The Minutemen were far outnumbered by the British soldiers, but the Minutemen had the advantage of knowing the terrain well. Because they were small in number, they were able to move quickly from one place to another. They couldn't defeat the entire British Army, but they certainly frustrated and angered a lot of British officers.

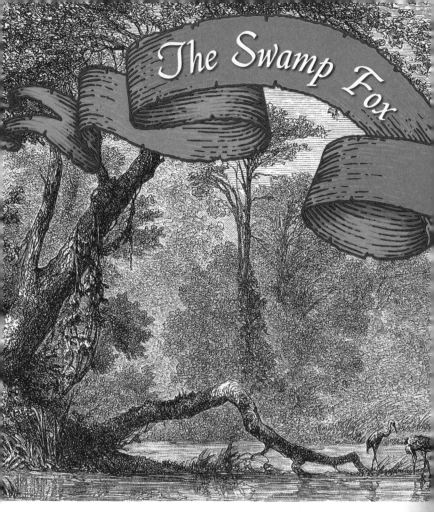

# The Swamp Fox

The men were hidden behind bushes, covered with leaves and standing behind trees in the South Carolina forest. They waited in silence, listening for the sound of boots marching on the ground. Then with a silent signal from their leader, Francis Marion, the soldiers attacked.

The British soldiers were stunned. Where was the army? Where were the uniforms? Who were they supposed to fight? It was guerilla tactics, and the British Army was totally confused.

Francis Marion was already 43 years old when the American Revolution started. He had spent 4 years fighting

> The soldiers who
> served with him
> were called Marion's
> Men, and they were
> all volunteers who
> received no pay
> and had to supply
> their own weapons,
> clothes, and food.

in the French and Indian War and learned to fight like the Cherokee did. He became a master at fast surprise attacks and taught his soldiers how to use the same skills.

The soldiers who served with him were called Marion's Men, and they were all volunteers who received no pay and had to supply their own weapons, clothes, and food. They were all dedicated to ridding South Carolina of the "scourge" of the British and they were loyal to their leader, the "old Swamp Fox."

Marion was called the Swamp Fox because of his ability to use the swamp areas of South Carolina to his advantage. Marion and his men knew the swamps and the British did not. When Marion and his men needed to escape, they would run into the swamps, and when the British followed, they would get lost. They could never find that "darned old fox."

The British never did catch Marion, and he is credited with helping to drive the British out of South Carolina. After the war, the Swamp Fox returned to his beloved plantation and spent the rest of his life as a farmer.

# Peter Francisco
## The One-Man Army

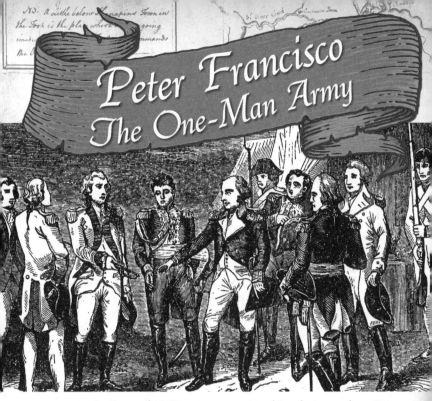

    In June of 1765, a very strange thing happened at City Point, VA. A foreign ship sailed up the James River and dropped anchor. Fishermen on the wharf watched as a long-boat was lowered into the water. Two sailors rowed the long-boat into the wharf and stopped only for a moment to hoist a bundle onto the dock. Then they rowed swiftly back to their ship, pulled anchor, and disappeared.

    Curious as to what the sailors had left, the local men ran to the dock. There they found a 5-year-old boy. He had a dark complexion, big brown eyes, and was wearing finely tailored clothing and shoes with expensive silver shoe buckles. He didn't speak a word of English. He tried to tell the people that his name was Pedro Francisco.

    The townspeople didn't know what to make of this strange event. It was obvious that the little boy came from a wealthy family who could afford finely tailored clothes, but the child was filthy and hungry, as though he had been on a long voyage. And who would abandon such a young child? They took Pedro to the local poorhouse to be cared for with the other orphans, but news of this strange event caught the attention of Judge Anthony Winston. Judge Winston took Pedro home to Hunting Tower Plantation and gave him a home, food, and work. He also changed the boy's name to Peter.

When Peter learned English, he was able to tell the judge what he remembered of his past, but it wasn't much. He remembered living in a large house near the ocean with lovely gardens. He also remembered playing in the gardens with his sister when rough men grabbed both of them. Peter's sister managed to get away, but Peter was tied up, gagged, and blindfolded. The next thing he knew, he was on a ship for a very long voyage.

The judge believed that Peter was from a wealthy family and had been kidnapped, probably for ransom, but something had gone wrong. Thankfully, the kidnappers had chosen not to kill Peter, but to abandon him at the wharf. During his lifetime, Peter never learned what happened to his family or where he was from.

Peter was a large child, and he grew into an even larger young gentleman. At the age of 15, Peter stood 6 feet 6 inches tall and weighed nearly 260 pounds. He was nearly a foot taller than the average man of the time. He was literally a giant among his peers. The judge had him trained as a blacksmith, which was an excellent job for such a strong boy.

When he was 14, he traveled with the judge to hear the judge's nephew Patrick Henry give his famous speech that ended with "I know not what course others may take, but as for me, give me liberty or give me death."

The words of that famous patriot influenced Peter to join the fight for colonial freedom. He wanted to enlist in the army, but the judge said he was too young. As soon as Peter turned 16, he enlisted as a private in the 10th Virginia Regiment.

He first saw battle at Brandywine Creek in Pennsylvania during September of 1777. Peter fought for General George Washington as they tried to stop the British from taking over Philadelphia. The battle was a disaster for the colonial rebels and Washington's troops had to retreat. Peter was one of the regiment who held the line at Sandy Hollow. They fought furiously for 45 minutes, working to protect the other troops as they withdrew. Peter was shot in the leg and was sent to a hospital in Bethlehem, PA.

While he was recovering, he met the Marquis de Lafayette who was then a 20-year-old general in Washington's army. The two young men hit it off and became fast friends, even though Peter was only a private.

Peter spent the next 3 years fighting for his adopted country. In the summer of 1779, he was hand-picked by General Washington to be one of 20 special commandos. Their assignment was to fight their way through a swamp in Redcoat territory, scale a 300-foot rock wall, and storm the British fort. Peter was the second man over the wall. During the fight, 17 of the commandos were killed and Peter took a 9-inch bayonet wound in his stomach. Although wounded, he still managed

## "GIANT" of a Stamp

In 1975, the U.S. Postal Service issued a stamp to **commemorate Peter Francisco and his brave acts**. It is a picture of Peter carrying the cannon out of the Battle of Camden.

to capture the Union Jack flag. He survived and went on to fight again.

The Battle of Camden in South Carolina did not go well for the American rebels. Once again they were in retreat, and once again, Peter was there fighting to save his comrades. Muskets were firing and bayonets were slashing, but through the haze and smoke Peter saw a British grenadier take aim at Colonial Colonel Mayo. Peter shot the grenadier and saved the colonel's life.

Immediately, several British soldiers tried to attack the giant soldier. Peter fought his way through the group of soldiers and threw one of them off a horse. Peter jumped on the horse and raced through the enemy lines, pretending he was a British soldier and shouting loyalist sayings as he rode away. He found Colonel Mayo and gave the horse to the exhausted colonel.

As he was marching away, Peter noticed that one of the Continental Army cannons was stuck in the mud. Peter didn't want the British to capture the cannon, so he took the 1,000-pound cannon out of its carriage and hoisted it into a horse-drawn wagon.

Peter continued to fight and was wounded six times, but he kept returning to the battlefield. His only complaint seemed to be that the sword he had was just too small to really fight with. He said it was like fighting with a toothpick. General Washington learned of Peter's complaint, and in March 1781, had a 6-foot broadsword delivered to Peter. He used this massive sword in the Battle of Guilford Courthouse in North Carolina. It was reported that he fought fiercely that day, taking out at least 11 Redcoats and suffering two serious wounds himself.

When British General Cornwallis surrendered at Yorktown, Peter was there. He joined his friend Marquis de Lafayette and witnessed the great event.

After the war, Peter decided he wanted to get an education, and that giant of a man did the bravest thing yet. He went to the local schoolhouse and squeezed his 6-foot, 6-inch body onto the

> **Want to know more about the "Giant of the Revolution"? You can watch a movie about Peter Francisco on YouTube: https://www.youtube.com/watch?v=3jRyxgip5ew**

small school bench, where he learned to read and write along with the local children. In only 3 years, he was reading classical literature. The children at the school loved Peter and always wanted to hear more of his stories from the war.

In 1784, Peter married Susannah Anderson. They settled in Virginia, and Peter became a farmer. Everyone told stories about the gentleman giant. They said he built his own house and carried the 14-foot logs by himself. They told about the time a man from Kentucky challenged Peter to a fight. Peter refused, and the man said he would not leave until Peter fought him. Peter simply tossed the man over a 4-foot tall fence and into a public road. But most people knew Peter as a kind man and a gentle "Virginia Giant."

In his later years, Peter was honored for his acts of bravery. In 1819, Congress awarded him a monthly pension for his service to his country, and 5 years later, he was honored to be visited by his old friend, the Marquis de Lafayette. And in 1825, Peter Francisco was named sergeant-at-arms of the Virginia Legislature. Peter died in 1831 at the age of 71 from appendicitis.

George Washington once commended Peter Francisco, saying, "Without him, we would have lost two crucial battles, perhaps the war, and with it our freedom. He was truly a one-man army."

# Smuggling for Freedom

General George Washington had a serious shortage of gunpowder. In 1775, there was only one American gunpowder mill and there was no way it could manufacture enough powder to supply an army. Without gunpowder, Washington's army was defenseless against the British. Washington did what any smart general would do: He ordered his troops to capture and smuggle in as much gunpowder as they could find.

Smuggling was nothing new to the colonists of America. They had spent years avoiding British taxes by smuggling goods into ports. Smugglers brought paper, tea, glass, and

Smuggling was nothing new to the colonists of America. They had spent years avoiding British taxes by smuggling goods into ports. Smugglers brought paper, tea, glass, and even paint to the colonists.

even paint to the colonists. England wanted to control the economy of the colonies, so they regulated what could be manufactured and even what other countries could sell to the Americans. Colonists saw nothing wrong with smuggling and believed that it was a necessary way of life. It was the only way they could get around the British laws without a war.

When war was declared, it ended the import of British gunpowder and weapons. The colonists set up their own manufacturing plants, but it was still not enough. The only way for them to get more gunpowder and arms was to buy them from smugglers.

Dutch and French tradesmen were only too happy to take the money offered by the colonists. They arranged to send shipments to ports where the British were not stationed and sometimes met at islands off the coast of the Americas.

Eventually the Continental Congress established the Committee of Secret Correspondence and a part of the committee's job was to secure the help of the French government. Long before the French officially agreed to help the colonists, they were sending shiploads of smuggled weapons and gunpowder.

Without the help of smugglers, General Washington would never have been able to fight the war and the United States of America might never have been become its own country.

# Founding . . . Smuggler?

**John Hancock, famous signer of the Declaration of Independence, was rumored to be a smuggler.** He was one of the wealthiest men in Massachusetts and ran a huge shipping business. Many people believed that he made his fortune smuggling tea to the colonists. The British charged him with smuggling and took him to court, but **his crafty lawyer, John Adams, got the charges dropped**. It was never proved that Hancock was a smuggler, but it is known what he did with most of his money—**he helped finance the war against Britain!**

# Sneaky Tricks

Spies of the American Revolution had it hard. No tiny spy cameras. Photography hadn't been invented yet. No recording devices, no telephones, not even a telegraph. What was a spy to do?

Get sneaky. Very, very sneaky.

During the revolution, spies had to use whatever means they had to hide themselves and their messages. Sometimes that meant inventing their own spy equipment and disguises. Spies disguised themselves as peddlers, cooks, farmers, and even wore the enemy's colors just to find out secret information. Once they got the information, they had to find a way to get it to their commander.

One way of sending a message was to hide it in plain sight. Every soldier carried a supply of musket balls. Spies carried a special silver ball the same size as the ammunition. This silver ball was hollow and could be opened up to hold a thin strip of paper. No one would ever check every single musket ball to see if the soldier was a spy, so it was an excellent hiding place.

It had an added advantage that it was small enough to swallow. If the spy was caught, he simply swallowed the silver ball and the evidence was gone. Then, after the ball made it through the spy's digestive tract, he could "retrieve" the metal ball and the message would still be safe and deliverable. Kind of gross, but it was effective.

Another way of passing a message was to hand the courier a feather. Today that would seem strange, but in George Washington's day, everyone used goose, swan, or turkey feathers as writing instruments. The metal-nibbed pen had not yet been invented. Quills were commonplace and that made them an excellent tool for spies. If a spy wanted to deliver a message, he would write it on a piece of paper using tiny printing. Then he would cut the paper into strips thin enough to fit inside a quill pen. Handing a quill pen to another person was nothing suspicious. It was a great way to deliver messages.

Buttons were another opportunity for hiding messages. Tiny slips of paper could be hidden inside metal buttons or under the cloth of homemade buttons. Nobody would be suspicious if a button fell off one soldier's jacket and it was picked up by someone else. All they had to do to read the message was to go to a private place and tear the button open.

SPY TRAINING

# Hidden Messages

You can be just as sneaky as the spies of the American Revolution. Look at some of the things you carry on a daily basis. There are lots of items you could use to hide messages. One of the easiest is a drinking straw. If you take a sack lunch to school, nobody would ever think to check your straw for a secret message.

## Materials

❏ Drinking straw

❏ Pen or pencil

❏ Scissors

❏ Writing paper

First, write your a message on the paper. Try to write a small as you possibly can.

Once you have written your message, cut it into thin strips. This not only makes it fit into the straw but it also makes your message like a puzzle so the reader will have to piece it back together. This makes it more difficult to read if somebody captures your message.

Then, slide the strips of paper into the drinking straw. Pack it in your lunch and you are ready to deliver the message. At lunch, just hand your partner the straw. Just warn him ahead time to look for your message **before** slurping his milk.

**SPY TRAINING**

# Swamp Training

The Swamp Fox and his men had to be sneaky and fast at the same time. You can train yourself to be as quick as the Swamp Fox with this game.

## Materials

- ❏ Several friends
- ❏ Chalk or masking tape
- ❏ 20 beanbags or small balls
- ❏ Referee

Using the chalk or tape, make two circles 50 feet apart. Divide your friends into two equal groups. Place an equal number of balls or beanbags in each team's circle. When the referee says "go," each team member takes a ball from her circle and tries to put it in the other team's circle. You run back and forth continuing to try to get all of the balls into your opponent's circle. When the referee yells "Stop," the team with the least number of balls in its circle is the winner.

# Bibliography

This political cartoon, attributed to Benjamin Franklin, originally appeared during the French and Indian War, but was recycled to encourage the American colonies to unite against British rule (from *The Pennsylvania Gazette*, May 9, 1754)

## Books

Allen, T. B. (2004). *George Washington, spymaster*. Washington, DC: National Geographic.

Beyer, R. (2005). *The greatest war stories never told: 100 stories from military history to astonish, bewilder, and stupefy.* New York, NY: Harper Collins.

Brinkley, H. (2012). *Spies of the American Revolution.* Hustonville, KY: HistoryCaps.

Daigler, K. A. (2014). *Spies, patriots, and traitors; American intelligence in the Revolutionary War*. Washington, DC: Georgetown University Press.

Davis, K. C. (2009). *America's hidden history: Untold tales of the first pilgrims, fighting women, and forgotten founders who shaped a nation.* New York, NY: Harper Perennial.

Fiske, J. (1981). *The American Revolution.* Boston, MA: Houghton Mifflin.

Kilmeade, B., & Yaeger, D. (2013). *George Washington's secret six: The spy ring that saved the American Revolution.* New York, NY: Penguin.

Nagy, J. A. (2010). *Invisible ink: Spycraft of the American Revolution.* Yardley, PA: Westholme Publishing.

Unger, H. G. (2011). *Improbable patriot: The secret history of Monsieur de Beaumarchais, the French playwright who saved the American Revolution.* Lebanon, NH: University Press of New England.

## Websites

American Merchant Marine at War. (2001). *Privateers and mariners in the Revolutionary War.* Retrieved from http://www.usmm.org/revolution.html

AmericanRevolution.org. (n.d.). *Artillery.* Retrieved from http://www.americanrevolution.org/artillery.html

Archiving Early America. (n.d.). *An eyewitness account of the Boston Tea Party as told by George Hewes.* Retrieved from http://www.earlyamerica.com/review/2005_winter_spring/boston_tea_party.htm

Archiving Early America. (n.d.). *A time for heroes: The story of Nathan Hale.* Retrieved from http://www.earlyamerica.com/review/2001_summer_fall/n_hale.html

BCW Project. (2011). *Soldiers of the civil wars.* Retrieved from http://bcw-project.org/military/units

Biography.com. (2014). *James Armistead.* Retrieved from http://www.biography.com/people/james-armistead-537566#synopsis

Biography.com. (2014). *Paul Revere.* Retrieved from http://www.biography.com/people/paul-revere-9456172#synopsis

Boston Tea Party Historical Society. (2008). *John Hancock— Smuggling powerhouse.* Retrieved from http://www. boston-tea-party.org/smuggling/John-Hancock.html

Boston Tea Party Ships and Museum. (n.d.). *The aftermath.* Retrieved from http://www.bostonteapartyship.com/the-aftermath

Crawford, A. (2007). *The swamp fox.* Retrieved from http:// www.smithsonianmag.com/biography/the-swamp-fox-157330429/?no-ist

Crews, E. (2004, Summer). Spies and scouts, secret writing, and sympathetic citizens. *Colonial Williamsburg Journal.* Retrieved from http://www.history.org/Foundation/journal/Summer04/spies.cfm

Dick, J. (2013). The gunpowder shortage. *Journal of the American Revolution.* Retrieved from http://allthings liberty.com/2013/09/the-gunpowder-shortage/

Durham, J. L. (1992). *Outfitting an American Revolutionary soldier.* Retrieved from http://ncpedia.org/history/usrevolution/soldiers

George Washington's Mount Vernon. (n.d.). *Spies, dead drops, and invisible ink: An interview with John Nagy.* Retrieved from http://www.mountvernon.org/george-washington/the-revolutionary-war/george-washington-spymaster/spies-dead-drops-and-invisible-ink/

George Washington's Mount Vernon. (n.d.). *Spy techniques of the Revolutionary War.* Retrieved from http://www.mountvernon.org/george-washington/the-revolutionary-war/george-washington-spymaster/spy-techniques-of-the-revolutionary-war/

Gray, M. (2007). James Armistead, Patriot spy. *TIME.* Retrieved from http://content.time.com/time/specials/packages/article/0,28804,1963424_1963480_1963442,00.html

Hickman, K. (2014). *American Revolution: Commodore John Paul Jones.* Retrieved from http://militaryhistory.about.com/od/naval/p/johnpauljones.htm

Klein, C. (2012). *10 things you may not know about the Boston Tea Party.* Retrieved from http://www.history.com/news/10-things-you-may-not-know-about-the-boston-tea-party

Lampson, C. R. (2011). *Privateers of the revolution.* Massachusetts Society Sons of the American Revolution. Retrieved from http://web.massar.org/privateers-of-the-revolution/

*Laodicea Langston: "Daring Dicey."* (n.d.). Retrieved from http://www.ezlangston.com/dicey.html

Legro, M. (2012). *From invisible ink to cryptography, how the American Revolution did spycraft and privacy-hacking.* Retrieved from http://www.brainpickings.org/index.php/2012/02/28/invisible-ink/

Library of Congress. (n.d.). *The George Washington Papers at the Library of Congress.* Retrieved from http://memory.loc.gov/ammem/gwhtml/gwtime.html

The Life of John Hancock. (2014). *The Liberty affair.* Retrieved from http://www.john-hancock-heritage.com/the-liberty-affair/

Longfellow, H. W. (1863). *The landlord's tale. Paul Revere's ride.* Retrieved from http://www.poetryfoundation.org/poem/173903

MacLean, M. (2009). *Dicey Langston.* Retrieved from http://www.womenhistoryblog.com/2009/04/dicey-langston-springfield.html

MacLean, M. (2009). *Women spies of the Revolution.* Retrieved from http://www.womenhistoryblog.com/2009/01/women-spies-of-revolution.html

*Mary Draper.* (n.d.). Retrieved from http://www.theamericanrevolution.org/peopledetail.aspx?people=53

McLaughlin, B. (2006). *Cornelius Drebbel: Inventor of the submarine.* Retrieved from http://www.dutchsubmarines.com/specials/special_drebbel.htm

Mohl, M. (2014). *Turtle.* Retrieved from http://www.navsource.org/archives/08/08441.htm

Moran, D. N. (n.d.). *Peter Francisco, giant of the American Revolution.* Retrieved from http://www.revolutionarywararchives.org/francisco.html

Naval History & Heritage Command. (n.d.). *"I have not yet begun to fight": The story of John Paul Jones.* Retrieved from http://www.history.navy.mil/trivia/trivia02a.htm

New York State Division of Military and Naval Affairs. (2006). *The American Revolution: A fight for freedom?* Retrieved from http://dmna.ny.gov/historic/articles/blacksMilitary/BlacksMilitaryRev.htm

Ouzts, C. (2005). *Nancy Hart (ca. 1735–1830).* Retrieved from http://www.georgiaencyclopedia.org/articles/history-archaeology/nancy-hart-ca-1735-1830

PBS. (2002). *World of influence: Spies.* Retrieved from http://www.pbs.org/benfranklin/l3_world_spies.html

Peter Francisco, Remarkable American Revolutionary War soldier. (2006). *American History Magazine.* Retrieved from http://www.historynet.com/peter-francisco-remarkable-american-revolutionary-war-soldier.htm

Ronemus, A. (1995). *Minutemen.* Retrieved from http://www.ushistory.org/people/minutemen.htm

Siniard, D. (2011). *Little known facts about the American Revolutionary War.* Retrieved from http://ncrevwar.lostsoulsgenealogy.com/revfacts.htm

*Spy letters of the American Revolution: Invisible ink.* (n.d.). Clements Library, University of Michigan. Retrieved from http://clements.umich.edu/exhibits/online/spies/methods-ink.html

Strauss, M. (2010). *Ten inventions that inadvertently transformed warfare.* Retrieved from http://www.smithsonian mag.com/history/ten-inventions-that-inadvertently-transformed-warfare-62212258/?no-ist

Thomas, H. (2014). *Chinese cannons history.* Retrieved from http://www.learnchinesehistory.com/chinese-cannons-history/

*Thomas Knowlton and his rangers: The taproot of U.S. Army intelligence.* (n.d.). Retrieved from http://huachuca.army.mil/files/History_MKNOWL.pdf

Valis, G. (2002). *Tactics and weapons of the Revolutionary War.* Retrieved from http://www.doublegv.com/ggv/battles/tactics.html

Wikipedia. (n.d.). *Boston Tea Party.* Retrieved from http://en.wikipedia.org/wiki/Boston_Tea_Party

Wikipedia. (n.d.). *Gunpowder artillery in the Song dynasty.* Retrieved from http://en.wikipedia.org/wiki/Gunpowder_artillery_in_the_Song_dynasty

Wikipedia. (n.d.). *Kate Barry.* Retrieved from http://en.wiki pedia.org/wiki/Kate_Barry

Wikipedia. (n.d.). *Minutemen.* Retrieved from http://en.wiki pedia.org/wiki/Minutemen

Wikipedia. (n.d.). *William Franklin.* Retrieved from http://en.wikipedia.org/wiki/William_Franklin

Williams, R. (2014). *Revolutionary War spy tools.* Retrieved from http://www.ehow.com/list_6930808_revolutionary-war-spy-tools.html

Woodward, A. (1861). *Memoir of Col. Thomas Knowlton of Ashford, Connecticut.* Retrieved from https://open-library.org/books/OL6525598M/Memoir_of_Col._Thomas_Knowlton

# About the Author

**Stephanie Bearce** is a writer, a teacher, and a history detective. She loves tracking down spies and uncovering secret missions from the comfort of her library in St. Charles, MO. When she isn't writing or teaching, Stephanie loves to travel the world and go on adventures with her husband, Darrell.

# More Books in This Series

Stealthy spies, secret weapons, and special missions are just part of the mysteries uncovered when kids dare to take a peek at the *Top Secret Files*. Featuring books that focus on often unknown aspects of history, this series is sure to hook even the most reluctant readers, taking them on a journey as they try to unlock some of the secrets of our past.

## Top Secret Files: The Civil War

The Pigpen Cipher, the Devil's Coffee Mill, and germ warfare were all a part of the Civil War, but you won't learn that in your history books! Discover the truth about Widow Greenhow's spy ring, how soldiers stole a locomotive, and the identity of the mysterious "Gray Ghost." Then learn how to build a model submarine and send secret light signals to your friends. It's all part of the true stories from the *Top Secret Files: The Civil War*.

ISBN-13: 978-1-61821-250-4

## Top Secret Files: World War I

Flame throwers, spy trees, bird bombs, and Hell Fighters were all a part of World War I, but you won't learn that in your history books! Uncover long-lost secrets of spies like Howard Burnham, "The One Legged Wonder," and nurse-turned-spy, Edith Cavell. Peek into secret files to learn the truth about the Red Baron and the mysterious Mata Hari. Then learn how to build your own Zeppelin balloon and mix up some invisible ink. It's all part of the true stories from the *Top Secret Files: World War I*.

ISBN-13: 978-1-61821-241-2

## Top Secret Files: World War II

Spy school, poison pens, exploding muffins, and Night Witches were all a part of World War II, but you won't learn that in your history books! Crack open secret files and read about the mysterious Ghost Army, rat bombs, and doodlebugs. Discover famous spies like the White Mouse, super-agent Garbo, and baseball player and spy, Moe Berg. Then build your own secret agent kit and create a spy code. It's all part of the true stories from the *Top Secret Files: World War II*.

ISBN-13: 978-1-61821-244-3